Silly

Silly is the way I feel when I make a funny face

and wear a goofy, poofy hat that takes up lots of space

For John

Emily

and Isabella

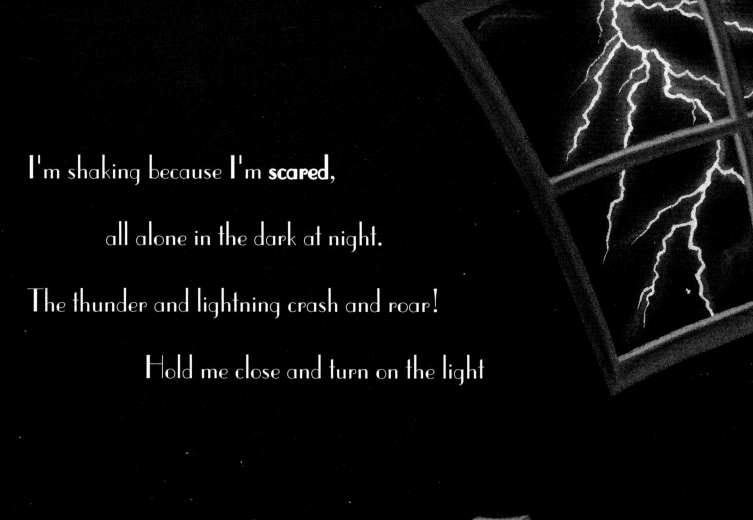

I'm shaking because I'm **scared**,

all alone in the dark at night.

The thunder and lightning crash and roar!

Hold me close and turn on the light

scared

The plans were made

so long ago

for you to visit

me today—

but now you can't

come after all.

I'm **disappointed**

we can't play

DISAPPOINTED

The smile you see upon my face as the sun shines in the sky shows the world that I feel **happy**, and my mood is soaring high

happy

Sometimes I feel

so very **sad**

and really

don't know why.

Instead of playing

and having fun,

I cry and cry

and cry

ANGRY.

"Angry is how I feel right now,"
I shout with a mighty roar.

I mostly want to frown and growl
and stomp upon the floor

Thankful

The wheel fell off my brand new truck—I needed some help from you.
You kindly fixed my favorite toy. I'm **thankful** for all you do

Frustrated

I'm **frustrated** because I can't do it.

It's hard and I want to cry.

I don't know whether to give it up

or to give it another try

shy

If someone

says "hello" to me,

I suddenly feel so **shy**.

Instead of waving

back at them,

I hide my face

and walk on by

I can't make up my mind— **bored**

there's nothing I want to do.

The day drags on and on.

I'm feeling **bored** and blue

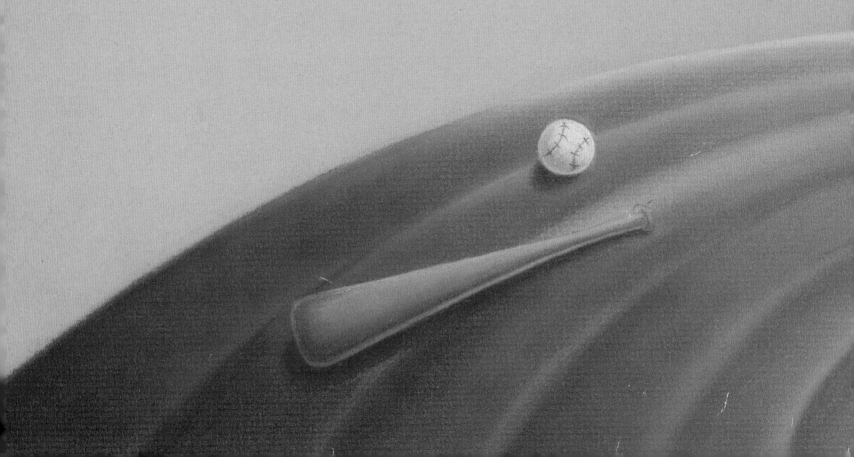

I'm bouncing like a rubber ball.

I'm more **excited** than I can say!

It's really hard for me to sit

When I'd rather jump and play

Excited

Jealous

I want to play with you right now.

I don't think taking turns is fair.

I'd rather have you to myself—

I'm **jealous** when I have to share

PROUD

"I did it! I did it!"
I shout to the crowd.
Getting dressed by myself
makes me feel **proud**

Feelings come and feelings go.
I never know what they'll be.
Silly or angry, happy or sad—
They're all a part of **me**!

A Note to Parents

Among my children's favorite books are word books.
My children love these books because, through words, these books give them language,
and through language, a better way to interact with the world around them. Emotions are an important aspect
of that world, yet few word books do for emotions what many word books do for the physical world.

In this spirit I have created **The Way I Feel**, a book designed to give children the language for their emotions.
My hope is that with language, children will be better equipped to understand and express their feelings.

In reading this book to your children, I'd like to offer these suggestions:

1

Ask your child what circumstances
make him or her feel happy, sad, jealous, and so on.

2

Discuss how to deal with emotions. ("If you're angry, it's not okay to hit or throw things,
but it is okay to stomp your feet....If you're sad, tell someone how you feel and ask for what you need.")

3

Talk about what actions or steps could be taken to change the circumstances
leading to a feeling your child doesn't like.

4

Practice noticing and naming feelings by asking your child how he or she feels at different times
throughout the day. Discuss the differences in emotions that may seem similar, such as
sad and bored, or jealous and mad, or happy and excited.

— Janan Cain

COMMUNITY RESOURCES FOR GERIATRIC PROGRAMS

A Practical Guide

ELLEN LEDERMAN, M.S., O.T.R.

Practical suggestions are provided in this book for finding, utilizing, and coordinating community resources to enhance the overall well-being of the elderly. Although activity programs provide a range of activities, the author maintains that it can be some time before geriatric participants interact with someone from the outside community. She stresses that community interaction is as crucial to the intellectual, social, cultural, and emotional welfare of the elderly as proper medication and medical/nursing care are to their physical health. Initial chapters focus on the need for, problems with, and solutions to expanding and utilizing community resources. Suggestions follow on where to locate these resources through the use of the Yellow Pages, community organizations, the public library, and local newspapers. Activity preparation work sheets are included in the final section to facilitate collection of data and coordination of activities.

CHARLES C THOMAS • PUBLISHER

Springfield • Illinois • U.S.A.

COMMUNITY RESOURCES
FOR
GERIATRIC PROGRAMS

COMMUNITY
RESOURCES
FOR
GERIATRIC PROGRAMS

A Practical Guide

By

ELLEN LEDERMAN, M.S., O.T.R.

CHARLES C THOMAS • PUBLISHER
Springfield • Illinois • U.S.A.

Published and Distributed Throughout the World by

CHARLES C THOMAS ● PUBLISHER

2600 South First Street

Springfield, Illinois 62717

© *1985 by* CHARLES C THOMAS ● PUBLISHER

ISBN 0-398-05077-5

Library of Congress Catalog Card Number: 84-16140

With THOMAS BOOKS *careful attention is given to all details of manufacturing and
design. It is the Publisher's desire to present books that are satisfactory as to their physical
qualities and artistic possibilities and appropriate for their particular use.* THOMAS
BOOKS *will be true to those laws of quality that assure a good name and good will.*

Printed in the United States of America

PS-R-3

Library of Congress Cataloging in Publication Data

Lederman, Ellen F.
  Community resources for geriatric programs.

  Bibliography: p.
  Includes index.
  1. Aged—Services for—United States. 2. Aged—Information services—United States. I.
Title. [DNLM: 1. Health Services for the Aged. 2. Community Health Services. WT 30
L473c]
HV1461.L39 1985   362.6   84-16140
ISBN 0-398-05077-5

For Mom and Dad

PREFACE

Community resources are one of the most valuable assets of any geriatric program. Unfortunately, meaningful interaction with the community at large is often very limited in many programs, centers, and facilities for the aged. This book attempts to offer practical suggestions for finding, utilizing, and coordinating resources within the community.

The first three chapters of this book provide basic background information. Chapter 1 discusses the very real and significant need for community resources in geriatric programs. In Chapter 2, some of the most prevalent problems regarding the utilization of community resources are discussed. Chapter 3 offers some tentative solutions to each of the problems.

The next three chapters feature practical suggestions for community resources. Chapter 4 describes the use of the Yellow Pages for locating individuals and groups who can offer their time and talents to geriatric programs. Chapter 5 details some of the ways in which public libraries can be utilized in the search for possible community resources. Chapter 7 outlines the way in which local newspapers can be a helpful adjunct to other means of finding appropriate community resources.

Chapter 8 contains a variety of activity preparation work sheets which can be used to organize data about community resources. Space is provided for the activity planner to record the name, address, and phone number of possibilities for community resources for the various activities. Suggestions are offered for materials and supplies, type of physical environment, number of participants, restrictions precluding participation, and types of outside participation to be solicited.

While no one volume can mention every possible community resource, it is hoped that this book provides a starting point for enhancing activity programs and a springboard for further development of creative approaches to community resources for geriatric programs.

CONTENTS

COMMUNITY RESOURCES
FOR
GERIATRIC PROGRAMS

Chapter 1

THE NEED

icture the typical geriatric program in a setting such as a day center or nursing home. What comes to mind is a large number of elderly people, some participating in activities offered within the setting, some chatting quietly with each other, some watching television, and others who are not involved at all in any sort of activity or socialization. Except for staff members and a few visitors, all the people in this scene are elderly. Most are from similar sociocultural backgrounds.

The significant element which is missing in this picture is the diversity of the outside world. In contrast with those of us who live in the outside community, the older people in the self-contained community lead lives within very restrictive boundaries, with almost no exposure to a variety of types of people and experiences. Such geriatric settings do offer safety, routine, and a sense of belonging, but the excitement, challenges, and stimulation of the real world are, far too often, almost completely missing.

The need for interaction with the outside community is a very real and important one, as important to the intellectual, social, cultural, and emotional well-being of the elderly as the proper medications and medical/nursing care are to their physical health. This essential interaction can be classified into two categories:

1. Interaction which maintains past ties, interests, and experiences.
2. Interaction which develops new interests and relationships, and provides new challenges.

Each of the two types can greatly add to the quality of the lives of the participants in geriatric programs.

Interaction Which Maintains Lifelong Associations and Interests

Throughout our lives, all of us are involved in relationships, organizations, and leisure interests. Such involvement assumes an important place in our lives. We would be reluctant to discontinue our involvement with them.

Elderly people have accumulated a lifetime of involvement with certain organizations, hobbies, and activities. Yet, all too often, they find themselves in an environment in which contact with these associations and interests is terminated. For example, the woman who has been a devoted member of her local garden club for thirty years becomes a resident of a nursing home which lacks any opportunity for continuing her interest in horticulture. The man who has attended weekly meetings of a club for people interested in creative writing attends a day program where no one else shares his interest.

All of us need, to varying degrees, some sense of order and security in our lives. Participation in familiar activities and groups helps to fulfill some of that need. Maintaining this participation thus becomes extremely important for elderly people who are forced to deal with the insecurity and trauma of a new environment, health problems, loss of a spouse or friends, and other factors.

Interaction Which Provides Opportunities to Develop New Interests and Relationships

As comforting as familiarity can be, we also need to experience new and different people, ideas, and activities.

Such experiences are what keeps life interesting, stimulating, and challenging. People who travel to foreign countries, scuba dive, or read a story which takes place in the distant past or future are all seeking an escape from their normal day-to-day existence.

This quest for new experiences does not suddenly terminate when a person reaches the age of sixty-five. While it is admittedly not an everyday occurrence for an octogenerian to decide to take up sky diving, there *are* thousands of older people who continue to seek new ideas and experiences through travel, literature, lectures, and just exploring all that the world has to offer.

Unfortunately, the vast majority of participants in a geriatric setting lead lives which are almost stifling in their monotony and predictability, while the outside community is full of interesting people and events. Interaction between the community at large and the population within a geriatric setting can be a mutually enriching experience for members of the community as well as the geriatric participants.

Chapter 2

THE PROBLEMS

Almost all geriatric programs utilize at least a few community resources. Members of the congregation of a local church might come to the facility to hold religious services; a pianist might volunteer her services once each month; and a group of volunteers might run the ubiquitous weekly bingo game. Nonetheless, the many possibilities for resources within the community are not being utilized to their maximum potential. Many geriatric programs lack variety and creativity in the utilization of local individuals and organizations.

There can be several problems in finding, developing, and utilizing community resources, but none are insurmountable. Their existence needs to be recognized and dealt with in an effective manner.

Lack of Time

The involvement of a large percentage of women in the work force has claimed a great deal of the time that used to be available for volunteer and civic work. The juggling of full time employment with familial responsibilities has drastically reduced the time that women can devote to other interests and activities. Working men also have limited time frames to accomplish maximum goals and responsibilities.

6

Lack of Awareness of the Need for Involvement With Geriatric Programs

The general public lacks awareness of the vital need for community involvement in geriatric programs. Since geriatric programs and facilities (i.e. day centers, retirement homes, and nursing homes) are generally isolated from the community at large, the rest of society tends to forget about these older citizens. Many geriatric institutions are located in geographically remote areas, far away from the turbulence of the center of city or suburban life. While these locations are tranquil and attractive, they also have the unfortunate by-product of removing older people from communities in which they actively participated for most of their adult life, thus contributing to the "out of sight, out of mind" phenomenon. Other nonresidential and residential facilities may be geographically within the community, but still not socially a part of the community.

Unless they actually have an older family member or friend who might be involved in a geriatric program, individuals who are interested in performing volunteer work might not even be aware of the presence of a geriatric program or facility within or nearby the community. Instead, such individuals volunteer their services at places such as schools and hospitals which have greater familiarity and visibility.

Lack of Incentives for Involvement With Geriatric Programs

Volunteering and sharing time, talents, and services is a noble deed, but it must be recognized that people do need incentives and rewards for such endeavors. The general public is often not aware of the intangible rewards that involvement with geriatric populations may bring.

Would-be volunteers may need some incentives for agreeing to and maintaining involvement in geriatric programs, just as volunteers at other kinds of programs and settings also need incentives for volunteering.

Lack of Real Understanding of the Needs of the Participants of Geriatric Programs

Well-meaning but ill-informed members of the community may have a limited understanding of older people, and impaired perceptions of the goals and purposes of geriatric programs. Some of the most common misconceptions and their consequences are listed below.

- Only very passive, sedentary activities are suitable for older persons.
  Consequently, members of the community who have interesting and unique talents or hobbies to share would never think of offering their services to a geriatric program.
- Older people often regress to childish behavioral patterns and should therefore be provided with activities suitable for children.
  Consequently, members of the community will provide entertainment and other activities which are demeaning to older persons, while neglecting to offer their services for relevant, age-appropriate entertainment and activities.
- Holidays are the most important time for volunteers to offer their services.
  Consequently, members of the community will remember geriatric populations once or twice a year on major holidays (i.e. Christmas) but neglect to offer their services at other times of the year.

Chapter 3

SOME SOLUTIONS

F inding, utilizing, and coordinating resources within the community is no easy task. It takes a great deal of creativity and perseverance to locate possibilities and persuade them that it would be worth their while to become involved in the geriatric program.

The previous chapter discussed the four most common problems encountered in developing community resources for geriatric programs. Some solutions are listed below.

Problem: Lack of Time

- Working people could volunteer their services at nights and on the weekends. Not all older people want to be in bed at seven o'clock or to watch television each night. Many would welcome lectures, visits, and other entertainment in the evenings.

- During the days, children are at school while young and middle-aged adults are at work. Older adults do not have these commitments and have more free time, both in general and, more specifically, in the daytime, than do other members of the community. With the over-65 population steadily increasing in the United States, older individuals constitute sizable reservoir of potential volunteers. The young-elderly and well-elderly population are significant community resources in programs for the old/frail/ fragile elderly population.

- Education is not restricted to school buildings. More and more schools are recognizing this fact and providing out-of-classroom experience for their students. Young people may have such busy after-school schedules that they don't have time for involvement with a geriatric program, but many would enjoy participating in the program as part of a class or school project. Teachers and administrators of local schools might be quick to recognize the value of interaction between students and the participants in a geriatric program. Many youngsters, especially if they live far away from their grandparents, never get a chance to really know their grandparents or any other older persons. Visiting with the elderly can provide firsthand and invaluable exposure to aspects of history, geography, economics, sociology, psychology, and foreign languages, enabling a more exciting learning experience than that which could be acquired from reading a textbook. Geriatric programs are also an excellent vehicle for college students to acquire actual experience in fields such as nursing, medicine, psychology, social work, health education, physical and occupational therapy, recreation, adult education, and, of course, gerontology. Furthermore, geriatric programs provide students of the fine/visual/ performing arts with an opportunity to perform or exhibit their talents in front of an enthusiastic and encouraging audience.

- Working people might be able to contribute their services to a geriatric program *on company time.* Some corporations are willing to let their employees lend their talents to worthwhile community endeavors while remaining on the company payroll for that period of time. For example, employees of one large corporation are allowed to help with civic projects up to four hours each month. Since such projects establish good will around the community, they are an excellent public relations tool for the company.

Problem: Lack of Awareness of the Need for Involvement With Geriatric Programs

Awareness of the need for involvement can be created through speeches to large groups and organizations. Many groups are amenable to having a representative from a geriatric program give a speech at their meetings. Possibilities include:

- Church and religious groups
- Women's organizations
- Men's organizations
- Civic and social service organizations
- Special interest and hobby groups
- Schools

Another means of creating public awareness of the needs of geriatric programs is through newspaper articles and news stories on television. Media coverage helps to acquaint the public with the existence and purpose of geriatric programs and facilities, as well as the possibilities for exciting activities and events. Such information can help to entice members of the community to become involved with a geriatric program. Therefore, every attempt should be made to procure media coverage for any event which could lend itself to an interesting story, in pictures, words, or both. In addition, such coverage is greatly appreciated by business people or organizations who would profit by having their names mentioned in media articles or stories, especially if it led to new customers or members.

Problem: Lack of Incentives for Involvement With Geriatric Programs

- One incentive for donating supplies and equipment to a geriatric facility (if nonprofit) is the tax deduction. Mileage to and from the program can also be claimed.
- Course credits could be given for participation if part of a class project.
- Badges for involvement could be given to Boy Scouts and Girl Scouts.

- If media coverage is obtained or if the event is advertised around the community, in terms of local newspapers or displayed signs, the person(s), organization, or business donating time, talent, and/or supplies will enjoy free advertising and, hopefully, more customers or members.
- Volunteer Recognition Days should be held several times a year. Some programs hold an annual volunteer luncheon, but it is recommended that they be held on a more frequent basis so that volunteers could be recognized and rewarded more consistently and regularly. Ideally, all community resources/volunteers who have donated their services during those months should be invited.
- Certificates of appreciation could be presented to each community resource after service is rendered. A regular weekly volunteer would not need a certificate each time he or she volunteers, but a certificate once every three to six months might be appreciated.

Problem: Lack of Real Understanding of the Needs of the Participants of Geriatric Programs

- The public needs to be educated about the capabilities of the elderly. Speeches to organizations who might be willing to get involved with geriatric programs could be helpful, as could media coverage of the many activities enjoyed by older persons. People need to be aware that completely passive, sedentary activities are not necessarily indicated for geriatric participants and, in many cases, not very beneficial to them.
- Many well-meaning individuals and groups offer their services to geriatric programs, but in inappropriate ways. Quite often, the activities they propose are not totally suitable for geriatric populations; many are too childish, while others are just too physically exhausting for the frail elderly. In such cases, it is crucial that only the *activity* gets rejected, and *not the individual or group* offering the activity. It is often possible to still retain much of the original flavor of the suggested activity while

slightly changing it to be more appropriate. If a church group offers to sponsor an Easter egg hunt for the geriatric participants and it is felt that this is not an age-appropriate activity, the activity can be slightly altered. An Easter egg hunt can still be held, but under somewhat different circumstances. The geriatric participants could hide the eggs and invite the children from the Sunday school class to find the eggs. This way, the church is still utilized as a community resource but not in a way which is demeaning or inappropriate for the elderly. Likewise, if an elementary school class decides that they would like to hold an aerobics session for the geriatric participants and it is felt that the children's understanding of the medical problems and cardiovascular capabilities of older people is so limited that they could not appropriately and safely instruct older people in exercise, this activity could still be used in a modified form. The children could perform an aerobics jazz dancing session in front of the audience without actually requiring the audience's physical participation. After the performance, the children could enjoy refreshments and conversation with their appreciative audience.

- Many would-be community resources and volunteers mistakenly believe that holidays are the most important time to volunteer their services, leading to an overload of resources and activities at certain major holidays and an unfortunate paucity during other times of the year. In fact, so many people are willing to volunteer to present special events at geriatric programs during holiday periods that many activity directors find that it is not possible to accommodate all of the volunteers. It can be logistically impossible to fit all those people who are willing to volunteer during the Christmas season into the month of December! On the other hand, other times of the year go begging for volunteers. A possible solution to the problem is the use of a "Christmas contract" in which individuals and groups pledge their services to a later date, thus spreading Christmas cheer throughout the year. For example, a group which wanted to entertain on a date close to Christmas might be willing to commit themselves instead to a date in March.

Chapter 4

THE YELLOW PAGES

The Yellow Pages of the local telephone book are an excellent means for finding possible community resources for geriatric programs. Almost all local businesses choose to be listed in the Yellow Pages, as does a significant number of nonprofit associations. Because the Yellow Pages offer such a comprehensive and readily accessible listing of what a community has to offer in the way of business, religious, social, cultural, and recreational resources, all individuals in charge of planning and implementing geriatric programs should take the time to become well acquainted with their directories.

The following pages offer a representative overview of listings which might be of interest to geriatric programs. The actual wording of the listings may vary from one locality to another. Different geographic regions have their own unique resources. Large metropolitan areas will have a larger and wider variety of resources than will a small rural town. Nonetheless, the majority of the resources listed in this section can be found in the Yellow Pages of most communities.

ACCOUNTANTS

Money is an important concern for most senior citizens. They are interested in learning how to invest their money so that they can conserve their capital assets and make them stretch as far as possible.

A financial seminar by an accountant can be helpful. The accountant can discuss investment strategies, tax information, and other financial information of interest to a geriatric population, such as:

- Estate Planning
- Trusts
- Wills
- Tax Tips for Over-65 Individuals
- Bonds
- Stocks
- Certificates of Deposit
- Ginnie Mae and Freddie Mac Investments
- Money Markets
- Bank Accounts
- Limited Partnerships

A question-and-answer period can be provided at the end of the speech. However, some individuals may be reluctant to ask questions and talk about their personal financial situation in front of an audience. Privacy can be protected by having the participants anonymously write down questions prior to the seminar. These questions can later be addressed by the accountant. Questions and concerns should be of general interest. Individuals with very specific, highly personal, or unique concerns could have the option of a private appointment with the accountant after the seminar on a fee-for-service basis.

Since this information can also be of interest to senior members of the community who are not involved in the geriatric facility or program, advance publicity for the seminar could be placed in local newspapers. Notices can be placed on bulletin boards in churches, grocery stores, and other places frequented by senior citizens in the community.

Follow-up activities may include small group discussions on personal finances, as well as a lending library of books on taxes, wills, trusts, investments, and budgeting.

TIP: Do not approach an accountant for such presentations during February through April. These are their busiest months because of income tax season!

ANTIQUES— DEALERS

Antiques fascinate almost everyone. A discussion and display of antiques can be interesting and informative.

Most antique dealers are very knowledgeable about the items they buy and sell. These dealers may be willing to bring some of their less valuable and less delicate antiques to the geriatric facility for a unique "show and tell" presentation. Program participants can listen to the lecture while given the opportunity to view the objects first-hand.

Some antique dealers specialize in certain artifacts such as old coins, Tiffany lamps, or Civil War memorabilia. In order to appeal to the greatest number of participants, it is recommended that the presentation be as varied as possible. While a few individuals may be highly interested in antique nautical items, for instance, others may be more excited about antique clothing, advertisements, furniture, toys, or political relics. A variety of items will ensure that each participant will find something of interest.

An hour-long lecture on antiques does have the potential to become boring. Audience participation greatly enlivens the event. Some of the participants (or their family members) may bring a favorite antique item and try to "stump the expert" by asking the antique dealer to guess its age and origin. Another alternative is to ask the audience, either as individuals or as teams, to guess the age and origin of the antiques. Prizes or awards may be given as appropriate.

Publicity of this event will be appreciated by antique dealers as it is a free advertisement for their businesses. Notices on community bulletin boards or in local newspapers may entice some of the outside community into attending the event. A large number of people of all ages are interested in antiques and may find such a presentation quite appealing.

Follow-up activities after the presentation may include displays of antiques in a lobby or other common area, as well as a small reading library on antiques.

ART GALLERIES, DEALERS, AND CONSULTANTS

A lecture on art appreciation can be intellectually and visually stimulating. Art dealers may be willing to bring in a number of paintings or other works of art (such as sculpture, ceramics, or weaving) to the facility.

Participants may be interested in hearing some personal information about the artists behind each work, such as when the artist was born, where he or she lived, and interesting aspects of his/her career. The art gallery owner or dealer can also explain and interpret each work.

Alternatives to gallery owners and dealers might include presentations by representatives of museums. It may also be possible to involve a high school or college class in the history, education, or appreciation of art. Students or teachers who are willing to undertake such a project may not be able to obtain original works of art by famous artists, but may be able to bring their own works or show slide presentations.

To generate excitement during the presentation, the audience may participate in contests or challenges. Some possibilities include:

1. After being shown representative works by several artists, the audience can be shown other paintings by the artists and try to guess which artist painted it. This can present quite a few surprises, especially if a certain artist markedly changed his or her style.

2. The audience may try to guess the national origins of the artists (i.e. which are American, French, Dutch).
3. The audience may try to guess the price of each painting. Many participants will be truly amazed at the high prices of most original works of art.

Members of the outside community who are interested in art might be invited to the event, via posters in libraries and notices in newspapers.

As a follow-up, some gallery owners might be willing to lend a different painting to be displayed each week in a prominent place. This can provide a broad exposure to a variety of artworks. A sign should be displayed with the name, address, and telephone number of the art gallery which is generously lending its art. This acknowledgement will be greatly appreciated by the owner, especially if it should result in new customers.

ART INSTRUCTION AND SCHOOLS

Teachers and students of the visual arts may be willing to share their time and talents. A variety of art classes may be found under the heading of "Art Instruction and Schools," as well as in high school and college art departments. These classes might include such media as oil paints, watercolors, pencil sketching, cartooning, sculpture, weaving, jewelry design, fashion design, or interior decoration.

Art students or their teachers may agree to give a demonstration of their expertise. If the artists are agreeable, audience members can watch and mingle with the artists-at-work.

One of the most enjoyable possibilities is a caricature or portrait session. Most people enjoy having a quick portrait done of themselves. Such portraits can be either in a serious or gently comic vein. Portraits or caricatures can be highly personalized if the subject is depicted in an activity or with an object that best typifies him or her. For example, the avid reader can be shown with his or her nose buried in a book.

Nominal purchase fees can help the artists to defray the costs of the art materials. For example, portraits can be purchased for a small price, as worked out with the artists so they can recoup the costs of the paper, ink, pastels, or pencils.

Advertising on community bulletin boards or in local newspapers can elicit a good response from members of the outside community who are interested in attending an art demonstration. Family members should be notified of the event, since a portrait of the entire family can be very meaningful.

Follow-up activities include a portrait gallery or other displays of the artists' work. Some participants may wish to try their hand at sketching, painting, or crafts, with the artists possibly coming back to give art lessons.

ASSOCIATIONS

Also listed under:

- Clubs
- Fraternal Organizations
- Social Service Organizations
- Youth Organizations

The Yellow Pages contain a partial listing of associations and clubs in the community. It must be noted that not all associations choose to spend the money to be listed in the Yellow Pages; consequently, many associations are listed only in the White Pages. The following list includes actual examples of listings found in the Yellow Pages of several different communities, along with brief suggestions on how to utilize the various associations.

Civic

Various civic groups may be willing to volunteer to be

friendly visitors, coordinate special events, or entertain. Many of these groups are listed under "Clubs" or "Fraternal Organizations."

- Elks
- Jaycees
- Kiwanis
- Knights of Columbus
- Lions Club
- Women's Clubs

Ethnic

Various ethnic groups may be willing to perform national dances and music, as well as to lecture and show films of their native lands.

- American Indonesian Friendship Council
- American Scottish Foundation
- Cuban Club
- Friends of Israel Alliance
- German Club
- Italian-American Society
- Japanese-American Society
- Polish American Society
- Swedish Club
- Swiss Society

Health

Health associations might be willing to lecture on relevant topics of physical and mental health.

- American Cancer Society
- American Lung Association
- Arthritis Foundation
- Association of Heart Patients
- Diabetes Association
- Mental Health Association
- National Kidney Foundation

Professional

Professional associations should be able to recommend and refer some of their members for lectures and other activities at the geriatric facility.

- Allied Health Professionals Association
  (physical therapy, occupational therapy, respiratory therapy, recreational therapy)
- American Osteopathic Disease Association
  (osteopathic medicine)
- American Society of Travel Agents
  (travelogues)
- Holistic Health Network
  (holistic health care)
- Institute of Certified Financial Planners
  (investments)
- Lawyer's Club
  (legal problems and their solutions)
- Pharmaceutical Association
  (proper use of medication)
- Podiatric Association
  (foot care)

Special Interest

Examples of the many possibilities include:

- Collector's Clubs
  Could show and lecture on a variety of collectibles.
- Mensa
  This club for persons of high intellect could furnish challenging intellectual games.
- Rare Gem Clubs
  Could exhibit and lecture on rare gems and minerals.
- Toastmasters or Toastmistress Club
  This club for the practice of public speaking could give interesting speeches.
- Writer's Club
  Could lead groups on creative writing.

ASTROLOGERS

Even people who don't really believe in astrology enjoy hearing their horoscopes and learning more about their astrological signs.

A person who is knowledgeable about astrology can give a lecture which focuses on such topics as future predictions of national and international significance, personality traits of each sign, compatible signs, and so on. Many participants also enjoy hearing the signs of famous people.

As a supplement to the lecture, it can be fun to have participants guess other people's signs, basing the guesses on what was learned from the lecture about the personality traits of each sign. Another possibility is the plotting of life charts of family members.

When talking about the future, it is important to keep all discussions as upbeat as possible. Gloomy forecasts such as the loss of a loved one or an injury or illness are not conducive to *anyone's* emotional health!

Advanced publicity should be posted in newspapers, on community bulletin boards, and in bookstores which specialize in the occult. Many members of the community are interested in astrology and might like to attend such a lecture.

As a follow-up activity, books on astrology should be made available. Horoscopes can be read on a daily basis to interested individuals.

ATTORNEYS

Senior citizens may have a myriad of legal concerns which need to be addressed by a lawyer. A practically-oriented legal seminar can be helpful to many persons. The attorney may discuss such subjects as:

- Consumer Issues, Including the Health Care System
- Estate Planning

- Housing Problems
- Investment Strategies
- Social Security
- Wills

A question-and-answer period can be provided at the end of the lecture. Some individuals may be reluctant to ask questions and talk about their personal legal situation in front of an audience. Privacy can be protected by having the participants anonymously write down questions prior to the seminar. These questions can later be addressed by the attorney. Questions and concerns should be of general interest. Individuals with very specific, highly personal, or unique concerns could have the option of a private appointment with the attorney after the seminar on a fee-for-service basis.

Publicity prior to the event could be placed in local newspapers or on bulletin boards in churches, grocery stores, and other places frequented by senior citizens in the community, since the legal information may be of interest to senior members of the community who are not involved in the geriatric program or facility.

Follow-up activities may include small group discussions on legal matters, as well as a lending library on legal matters.

AUCTIONEERS

Auctions can be great fun. A professional auctioneer may be willing to donate his or her services for an auction at the geriatric facility. While the auctioneer might conduct the session with items similar to those typically sold at regular auctions, a better alternative is to have him or her auction items which have been donated by the staff, family members, and the participants themselves. If there are not enough donations, merchandise could be bought and then sold at a profit. Money made at this event could later be used towards other special events and functions in the geriatric program.

Possible items to be auctioned include:

- Artworks and Craft Items
- Baked Goods
- Books
- Clothing
- Furniture
- Gift Items
- Jewelry
- Perfumes
- Plants
- Records
- Services such as Calligraphy, Babysitting, Hair Styling, Sewing or Tailoring

Every attempt should be made to include the general public. Posters and other means of advertising should be displayed all around the community. Advertisements may appear in newspapers and on the radio.

A committee might meet on a regular basis to create and collect items to be auctioned at a later date.

AUDIOLOGISTS

Since a significant percentage of people over the age of sixty-five have hearing problems, a lecture by a professional audiologist can be relevant. The discussion can include such topics as:

- The Anatomy and Physiology of the Ear
- Common Auditory Problems of the Elderly
- Solutions to the Problems, Including Hearing Aids

It may be possible for the audiologist to actually perform audiological testing or demonstrate the use of hearing aids. In the case of testing or fitting with hearing aids, it may be wise or necessary to get a physician's referral or prescription.

Audiologists in private practice will appreciate publicity of their lecture. Appropriate means include newspapers, community bulletin boards, and doctor's offices.

BAKERS—RETAIL

See Also Cake Decorating

Watching a professional baker at work can be quite enjoyable. It may be possible to arrange for a baker to come to the geriatric facility and demonstrate his or her craft. The preparation of a variety of baked goods (such as sculpted breads, fancy cakes and cookies) could be demonstrated. If possible, some of the audience could help with the preparation under the baker's instruction. In some cases, the baker might not actually bake the items at the facility, but could bring finished products that are similar to those which were prepared during the program. Participants almost invariably want to sample the end products of their work!

Another possibility is for the participants to compete in a "bake-off" contest. Cakes and other baked goods could be made prior to the contest. The baker could serve as the judge, awarding a prize for the best cake.

To help defray the costs of the ingredients for the baker, a baked goods sale could be held after the demonstration. Many staff members will want to purchase the baked goods, as may some of the participants for their families and friends. Publicity in newspapers and on community bulletin boards will ensure a good response from the public. If a profit (over and above the actual costs) is made, it can be utilized for other events.

Follow-up activities include baking classes and bake sales.

TIP: Diabetic participants need to be carefully supervised to avoid sampling of restricted desserts.

BARBERS
BEAUTY SALONS
and
BEAUTY SCHOOLS

Professional or student beauticians may be willing to come to the geriatric facility and donate services such as:

- Hair Coloring
- Hair Cutting
- Hair Styling
- Makeup Application
- Permanent Waving
- Skin Care

Even if the beautician is willing to donate his or her services, the geriatric program or individual participants should be responsible for paying for the cost of supplies, such as the permanent lotion or hair color.

Another possibility is a lecture/demonstration on beauty tips for mature women. The lecturer could discuss hair and skin care, appropriate hair styling, and makeup application.

A beauty group could be scheduled on a regular basis. Group members could practice hair styling or makeup application on themselves or each other.

BARTENDING SERVICES
and
BARTENDING SCHOOLS

The enjoyment of alcoholic beverages does not automatically end when individuals reach their sixty-fifth birthdays. Physicians are increasingly likely to advocate a glass of wine with dinner or a nightly cocktail.

A lecture/demonstration by a professional bartender or bartending students can be a very enjoyable activity. The bartender can explain and mix a variety of exotic drinks, many of which might be unfamiliar to the audience. After each drink is mixed, it might be offered to a member of the audience to try. Hors d'ouevres might complete the "cocktail party."

While some bars, lounges, and restaurants might be willing to provide the liquor, others will not. Free-lance bartenders will usually not be able to provide any liquor, so the activity program might need to underwrite the cost of the event.

The atmosphere for this activity should be congenial and intimate, promoting socializing among participants, so it will generally not be appropriate to solicit participation from members of the community, but staff members and the families of the participants might be invited. When possible, media coverage of the event might be appreciated by the bartender or owners of the bartending school/lounge/restaurant donating the services.

As a follow-up to the event, cocktail parties can be held on a regular basis, with some of the participants serving as bartenders.

TIP: A doctor's approval (or formal prescription) usually needs to be obtained prior to serving alcoholic beverages, but this is usually not a problem. Most physicians now recognize that a moderate intake of alcoholic beverages can be beneficial to the over-65 population.

BEER: HOME BREWING EQUIPMENT AND SUPPLIES

Many people enjoy drinking beer. The over-65 population is no exception, yet they are often denied opportunities to indulge in drinking the golden brew.

Owners or managers of retail stores which sell equipment, supplies, and instruction on how to brew beer at home may be willing to provide a demonstration on the art of beer brewing. Because the actual process takes about six weeks until the beer is ready for consumption, the instructor will not be able to let the participants sample the brew on the spot, but he or she may be able to bring in some beer that was previously brewed and is now ready. The brew made that day may be left at the facility so that participants can bottle it at a later date, and finally imbibe a few weeks later.

The actual costs of the supplies and equipment for beer making can be recouped by letting interested participants purchase the beer for consumption or to allow staff members to purchase the beer to take home, as homemade beer is much less expensive than that which is available in stores.

Publicity for the event (in newspapers and on bulletin boards around the community) may result in drawing members of the community into the facility to learn how to brew their own beer. The owner of the store which sells beer-making supplies will be grateful for any publicity which results in more customers.

Follow-up activities include finishing the brewing process and experimenting with the brewing of different types of beer.

TIP: A doctor's approval (or formal prescription) usually needs to be obtained prior to serving alcoholic beverages, but this is usually not a problem. Most physicians now recognize that a moderate intake of alcoholic beverages can be beneficial to the over-65 population.

BIOFEEDBACK THERAPISTS

Psychologists, physical therapists, and other professionals are becoming interested in the use of biofeedback to improve physical and mental health. Through psychological methods such as relaxation training and mechanical means such as electromyographic techniques, it is possible to reduce stress, muscle tension, and pain.

A biofeedback therapist may be willing to conduct a lecture/demonstration session at the geriatric facility. Although the techniques are generally quite innocuous, it is best to procure a physician's approval before enrolling each individual in the session.

Because small group settings are the most conducive to this event, publicity does not need to be posted around the community.

As a follow-up, relaxation training groups may be held on a regular basis.

CALLIGRAPHERS

Fancy lettering by hand is an art form which many people enjoy. It is an exacting process, but the results are gratifying.

Professional calligraphers may be willing to demonstrate their craft. The audience may enjoy watching the calligraphers letter their names onto small strips of paper to serve as an attractive nameplate.

If possible, audience participation should be encouraged. Participants may (under the guidance and instruction of the calligrapher) try their own skill at lettering. If the calligrapher is unable to provide the pens, ink, and paper, these supplies will need to be obtained prior to the demonstration and practice session. To generate excitement, a contest may be held in which the best attempt (as determined by the calligraphy instructor) receives a prize. An appropriate prize may be an elaborately lettered plaque or scroll.

This activity is best as a small group event. Outside participation does not need to be elicited.

The participants may wish to continue to pursue calligraphy. A calligraphy group can serve many useful functions; some of these include lettering headings on the program's or facility's newsletters, and lettering invitations for future events. With practice, some of the participants may gain enough skill to do professional calligraphy, hiring out their services to the outside community for their wedding announcements, invitations, certificates, and so on.

CAKE DECORATING—EQUIPMENT AND SUPPLIES

The decorating of cakes and other baked goods is truly an art. Many geriatric participants enjoy watching a cake decorator at work. The owner of a business which sells supplies and provides instruction in cake decorating may be willing to demonstrate all the amazing possibilities of his or her craft.

The cake decorator may agree to provide the cakes or the facility may provide some undecorated cakes. Hands-on instruction may enable some of the participants to actually decorate the cakes themselves. Cake decorators often have photographs of some of their "masterpieces," which they can circulate around the audience. Participants may wish to sample some of the finished products to see if they taste as good as they look!

To help defray the costs of the cakes for the decorator or the facility, a baked goods sale can be held after the demonstration. Many staff members will want to purchase the cakes, as may some of the participants for their family and friends. Adequate publicity in newspapers and on bulletin boards in grocery stores and churches will ensure response by the public, thus adding to the sales and promoting social interaction. It may even be possible to make a profit (over and above the actual costs) which can be utilized for other events.

Follow-up activities include baking classes and bake sales.

TIP: Make sure that diabetic participants are carefully supervised to avoid sampling of restricted desserts.

CANDY MAKING (SUPPLIES AND MOLDS)

Making candy is almost as enjoyable as eating it! Candy making is not a new activity. Throughout the years, people have always made homemade candy. What's changed is the ease and convenience with which candy can now be made.

The owner or manager of a retail business which sells supplies and provides instruction in candy making may be willing to demonstrate the art of candy making. Hands-on instruction may enable some of the participants to actually decorate the cakes themselves. In addition, photographs of some of the most unique creations (i.e. houses, tennis rackets, cars, pianos, all made of chocolate or other sweets) may be circulated around the audience. It will be difficult for participants to avoid the temptation of sampling the finished products!

To help defray the costs of the candy, a candy sale can be held after the demonstration. Many staff members and geriatric participants will want to purchase candy for their family and friends. Adequate publicity in newspapers and on community bulletin boards will ensure public response, thus increasing sales and promoting social interaction with the program members. It may even be possible to make a profit (over and above the actual costs) which can be utilized for other events.

Follow-up activities include:

- Candy making classes in which students may try their hand at other types of candy. (Although most candy makers concentrate on chocolate, participants may also enjoy such old-fashioned experiences as taffy pulls.)
- Candy sales.
  Distribution of candy to children at day care centers or to children who visit the facility or program.
- Reading library on candy making and chocolate.

TIP: Make sure that diabetic participants are carefully supervised to avoid sampling of restricted candy.

CERAMIC PRODUCTS (SUPPLIES AND INSTRUCTIONS)

A ceramics instructor may be willing to donate some greenware (free of charge or at a nominal cost) to the geriatric program, as well as instruction in painting and decorating the greenware. Arrangements will have to be made to transport the decorated pieces between the facility and the ceramics studio as they will need to be fired in the studio's kiln.

A small group session is most appropriate for this event, so publicity around the community is not necessary.

Arrangements may be made with the ceramics studio to hold the ceramics classes at the facility on a regular basis. The program could purchase the greenware from the studio in return for the use of its kiln.

CHINESE FOOD PRODUCTS

Most retail stores which specialize in Chinese food products are owned and operated by individuals who either are Oriental or highly interested in Chinese cooking. Such cooking (especially stir frying) is a unique way of preparing food and is a type of cooking in which many people over sixty-five have had little or no experience. A demonstration of Chinese cooking by a knowledgeable individual can be fascinating.

Experienced Chinese cooks may be able to bring several woks to the facility, along with other cooking paraphernalia and foodstuffs. Participants will enjoy watching this quick and dramatic style of cooking. They will especially enjoy sampling the end product!

Most cooks will greatly appreciate partial or full reimbursement of the cost of the foods. They will also appreciate publicity of the event, as it may help to generate new business. Publicity also helps to entice family and other members of the community to attend the event.

Follow-up activities include Chinese cooking classes in which participants can actually prepare the food themselves.

TIP: Before allowing participants to sample the food, it must be ascertained that the food does not violate any dietary restrictions. It is also wise to make sure that food prepared by an outside source (rather than inside the facility's own kitchen by its staff) does not violate any health codes.

CHIROPRACTIC PHYSICIANS

A chiropractor may be willing to lecture at the geriatric facility. Appropriate topics may include:

- Nutrition
- Proper Body Mechanics
- Stress Management
- The role of the chiropractor in treating certain illnesses which occur in older persons.
- Use of physical agents such as water, cold, or massage for relief of pain and muscle tension.

Since the lecture might be of interest to other people in the community, publicity for the event should be posted in newspapers, in the chiropractor's office, and on bulletin boards around the community.

Books on chiropractic and associated topics could be made available to interested participants.

CHURCHES AND SYNAGOGUES

Church groups are among the most valuable assets of any geriatric activity program. From children's groups to adult groups, many church members are interested in providing a variety of services to the elderly, either as formal group projects or on an individual, informal basis. Involvement may range from a one-time special program to continuing visits on a regular basis.

By calling the church or temple office, it is possible to contact the minister, pastor, priest, or rabbi, or the heads of the women's or children's groups. The response from these groups can be very gratifying.

Some of the many possible ways to utilize church groups are listed below.

1. Entertainment

Children, adolescents, and adults can provide entertainment such as singing, dancing, and acting, depending on the skills and talents of the members. Programs can be either religious or secular. In many cases, church choirs are extremely talented and the beauty of their music can be enjoyed by many individuals, even those who hold differing religious beliefs. The entertainment may be general in nature or may relate to a specific religious holiday (such as Easter) or a nonsecular holiday (such as Mother's Day). Some churches are largely composed of members with unique national origins, such as Greek Orthodox churches; Catholic churches with a significant membership of Hispanic individuals; or places of worship for Oriental persons. Such congregations may be willing to present a program which reflects their ethnic heritage (i.e. Greek folk dancing, Latin music, or Japanese tea ceremonies).

2. Visitation Programs

Each member of a congregation may "adopt" one geriatric participant in an "Adopt a Grandparent" program and visit their adoptive grandparent on a regular basis. It is important to ensure that such visitations do occur on a regular basis, be it weekly or every other month. If relationships develop and then are irregularly continued, the adopted grandparents will be extremely disappointed. If the church group is unable to commit itself on a regular enough basis for the "Adopt a Grandparent" program, they can still provide occasional social visitations in which they mingle with the entire geriatric population of the facility.

3. Conducting or Assisting With Religious Services and Bible Study

Some facilities are not fortunate enough to have the active involvement of a priest, minister, or rabbi. Members of a congregation may be willing to provide worship services on a regular basis to the residents of the geriatric facility or the clients of a geriatric program.

4. Pen Pal Program

A pen pal program may be developed between the participants of the geriatric program and the members of a church group, thus enabling the participants to receive mail.

5. Provision of Supplies

Some church groups have members who (for reasons of health, time, or transportation restrictions) are unable to actually participate in the program, but would still like to contribute something, such as handmade gift items. Other church groups may be willing to collect and contribute craft materials, magazines, books, and objects to be used for prizes or gifts.

COINS—DEALERS AND SUPPLIES

Coin collecting can be an interesting hobby. A number of geriatric participants might have collected foreign or antique coins at some point in their lives. Even those who are totally unfamiliar with coin collecting might still enjoy a lecture on various coins. Learning about the history behind each coin can be fascinating. Individuals who work in coin stores are usually quite knowledgeable about coins and might be willing to bring a variety of them to the geriatric program. Whenever possible, coins should be circulated around the audience so that the participants can get a close look at the coins.

History or social studies classes from a nearby school might be invited to attend the lecture.

Books on coin collecting should be made available to interested readers. A coin collecting group might wish to meet on a regular basis.

COLOR CONSULTANTS

Several years ago, Carole Jackson wrote a book entitled *Color Me Beautiful* which addressed the important role that color plays in our lives. She postulated that each of us looks best in certain color families. Knowing and using our "ideal" colors can make us look and feel our best. This concept has become quite popular, leading to other books about color and color consulting businesses.

A color consultant may be willing to provide a lecture/ demonstration. The main color groups could be discussed, followed by information on how to find one's own best colors. A visual demonstration should be included. The color consultant could demonstrate the difference that "right" or "wrong" colors make by holding different swatches of fabric up to the faces of the participants, using different colors of makeup, or having the participants model clothing in various colors.

For maximum audience participation, it can be fun to hold a contest to guess which colors are best for each individual. A prize could be awarded to the participant with the greatest number of correct guesses. Another interesting variation is to see if the participant's favorite colors are the same as those which the color consultant believes are the best ones for that person.

As a business person, the color consultant will probably appreciate publicity about the event. Advance notice could be placed on bulletin boards around the community or in newspapers, inviting interested members of the community to attend. This is also an ideal event to photograph. Before and after pictures of the participants could show the effect of different colors. These photographs could then be displayed in a prominent place at the facility, along with the color consultant's business card or a sign with his/her name and phone number.

Follow-up activities may include discussion groups in which the participants continue to explore the use of colors. A paperback copy of one of the books on color can be made available to participants who wish to read about the subject.

COMPUTER PROGRAMMING SERVICE
COMPUTERS—DEALERS

Many older persons have had little, if any, exposure to computers. A demonstration of some of the functions and abilities of computers can be truly fascinating for geriatric populations.

Computer salespeople from retail outlets or computer programmers may be willing to bring computers to the facility for a lecture/demonstration ranging from such topics as stock market analysis to computer games to basic functions. Participants should be given an opportunity to actually try the computer.

While advance publicity could be posted on computer bulletin boards, in all likelihood, most members of the community will not be interested in attending this computer seminar since most are already familiar with computers or can easily learn about them at school, work, or computer stores. However, local newspapers may be interested in taking some photographs of the participants as they experience the computer age.

As a follow-up activity, books on computers could be made available for personal reading. Some participants may wish to gain more expertise on personal computers.

COOKING INSTRUCTION

Cooking lessons can be an enjoyable activity for both men and women. Most communities have a variety of cooking classes offered on a regular basis, ranging from French gourmet to Chinese vegetarian cuisines.

A demonstration by a cooking instructor can be very entertaining. People generally enjoy watching a master chef at work, describing his or her techniques while creating culinary delights. Naturally, sampling the finished products adds to the enjoyment! Whenever possible, the cooking instructor can allow actual participation by the audience.

In most instances, partial or full reimbursement of the cost of the food will be appreciated by the cooking instructor. Publicity of the event will also be appreciated, as it may help to generate new business.

Follow-up activities include cooking groups held on a regularly scheduled basis.

TIP: Before allowing participants to sample the food, it must be determined that the food does not violate any dietary restrictions. It is also wise to make sure that food prepared by an outside source (rather than inside the facility's own kitchen by its staff) does not violate any health codes.

COSTUMES—MASQUERADE AND THEATRICAL

Businesses which buy, sell, rent, or manufacture costumes for masquerade parties and theatrical productions may be willing to lend costumes to the geriatric program.

A costume party can be an enjoyable event. If the lender is willing, some participants may wish to dress in full costumes, whereas others may only want to wear accessories, such as hats. A costume show may be held, utilizing both staff members and geriatric participants as models. Employees of the costume store may also be willing to serve as models. The selected costumes may have a specific theme such as the Roaring Twenties or may be eclectic in nature, with one costume having little to do with another.

Contests are a possibility. Prizes may be given for the prettiest or funniest costumes, or for the person who makes the greatest number of correct identifications of the persons, objects, or periods of time represented by the costumes.

Since this is a highly visual event, it may be possible to arrange for newspaper coverage. This can be mutually advantageous for the geriatric program and the costume store, since it provides publicity for both. The public may also be invited to observe the event.

As a follow-up activity, participants may enjoy creating costumes themselves for a future party.

COSMETICS AND PERFUMES—RETAIL

Cosmetics and perfumes are enjoyed by most individuals, including those who are over the age of sixty-five. A makeup session can be a definite morale booster.

Many of the stores, companies, and representatives which sell cosmetics may be willing to donate samples of cosmetics, perfumes, and various sundries. Some are also willing to provide lectures and demonstrations which pertain to their products. Possibilities include:

• Makeup Lessons
• Makeup Applications
• Facials
• Lectures about the Use of Perfume
• Testing and Sampling of Various Perfumes
• Lectures about Skin Care

Sources include cosmeticians at drug stores, beauty salons, and cosmetic studios, as well as representatives of national companies such as Mary Kay or Avon. After the session, the cosmetician or representative may wish to make available some cosmetics and perfumes for purchase. (Care should be taken to ensure that participants are not pressured into buying items.)

The actual number of participants should be kept low enough to enable all to partake in the makeup application or facials, although some may prefer to observe rather than participate.

Follow-up activities may include:

- A lending library of books dealing with cosmetics.
- A "store" within the facility which sells cosmetics and perfumes. This may be held as often as twice a week or as seldom as every other month, depending on the demand.
- A grooming or makeup group held on a regular basis.

COSMETICS—WHOLESALERS AND MANUFACTURERS

Many wholesalers and manufacturers are willing to donate samples of cosmetics and perfumes, although they may not be able to provide any personnel who can demonstrate makeup application. The donated samples may be utilized in makeup and grooming groups or for prizes for bingo and other games and contests.

COUNSELORS—HUMAN RELATIONS

Also listed under:

- Psychiatrists
- Psychologists
- Social Workers

A professional counselor may be willing to lecture on various aspects of human relations and self-coping. The topics should be geared towards the areas which most concern geriatric populations. Examples include:

- Adjusting to the Loss of a Spouse
- Coping With Congregate or Institutional Living Environments
- Coping With Illness
- Dealing With Death and Dying
- Dealing With Neglect or Overprotection From Family Members
- Handling Conflict
- Stress Management

A question-and-answer period may be held at the end of the session. Some individuals may be reluctant to ask questions and talk about their human relations problems in front of an audience. To ensure privacy, participants may anonymously write down pertinent questions prior to the seminar.

Advance publicity for the lecture could be placed on church bulletin boards and other public places.

Follow-up activities may include small group discussions on human relations and on coping with various difficulties, as well as a lending library of books on social and psychological topics.

CRAFT INSTRUCTION

Stores which sell craft supplies usually provide instruction in such crafts as:

- Needlepoint
- Embroidery
- Rug Hooking
- Decoupage
- Stained Glass
- Jewelry Making
- Ceramics
- Paper Quilling
- Knitting
- Crocheting
- Soft Sculpture
- Bunka
- Quilting

These stores may be willing to provide instruction on either an introductory or continuing basis. To ensure an adequate number of participants, the craft store may wish to display a sign and use a sign-up list for customers of the store who might wish to attend. Publicity could also be posted in newspapers and on bulletin boards in adult schools and community centers, nearby apartment complexes, churches, and shopping centers.

As a follow-up, craft groups could continue to meet, even if the professional instructor is not available. A staff member or geriatric participant may have learned enough from the craft instructor to take over the leadership of the group. A lending library could contain books on various craft projects.

DANCING INSTRUCTION

Schools which provide instruction in dance may be willing to get involved in a geriatric program.

One possibility is for the dance students to give a recital at the geriatric facility, provided the facility can furnish an appropriate space for the performance. Types of dance might include ballroom, ballet, jazz, tap, and modern.

Another possibility is for the instructors at the dance studio to showcase their own talents by performing. Such shows can be very exciting and enjoyable.

Still another possibility is for the students and instructors to give dance lessons to members of the audience. Ballroom dancing is the most appropriate type of dancing for ambulatory participants. This can be made into quite a gala event, with participants dressing at least semiformally. For nonambulatory, wheelchair-bound participants, it may be possible for the students/instructors to adapt modern dance or ballet techniques for the upper extremities.

In most instances, dance studios will appreciate publicity for the event. The dance lessons or recitals lend themselves very well to photographic coverage from the newspaper or television news. Advance publicity for the event (i.e. on community bulletin boards or in newspapers) may entice some members of the community into attending. Parents or friends of student performers may be invited to attend the recital and mingle with the geriatric members of the audience after the performance.

Follow-up activities may include a continuing dance/movement group.

DAY NURSERIES AND CHILD CARE

Directors of child care centers may be interested in bringing the children to the geriatric program on either an occasional or regular basis. If visits are not to be scheduled on a regular basis, the children could come once or twice a year to entertain with short skits or songs.

Whenever possible, a good relationship between the child care center and the geriatric program should be developed. Recent research has demonstrated the significant value of such interaction for both age groups. Programs can range from unstructured, informal visits to planned events, such as preschool children's games in which each child is paired with a "grandparent."

Ideally, visits are scheduled on a regular, frequent basis. When this is not possible, the elderly participants may correspond with their young friends by mail.

DENTISTS

Dentists may be willing to provide an informative lecture on aspects of dentistry which concern the elderly. The two specialties with the greatest relevance for geriatric populations are periodontics (gums and soft tissues) and prosthodontics (dentures).

A question-and-answer period may be conducted at the end of the session.

The dentist may wish to post a sign in his or her office to inform current patients who might be interested in hearing their dentist speak. Most dentists would appreciate other publicity (i.e. newspapers or notices on community bulletin boards) since it could result in attracting new patients.

Follow-up activities might include a library with books or pamphlets on dental care.

DOLLS—REPAIRING
and
DOLL HOSPITALS

Individuals who work for or own a doll "hospital" can provide an interesting lecture and exhibit. Many of the dolls which they own or are in the process of repairing are truly fascinating. Some are antiques, whereas others are from foreign countries or just very unusual.

The lecture should be approximately forty-five minutes in length, focusing upon the historical or cultural aspects of each doll. Ideally, the dolls should be presented to the audience during the lecture; if this is not possible, they may be displayed afterwards.

Because this event may be equally enjoyed by individuals of any age, grandchildren and other relatives of the participants could be invited. Elementary school classes or Brownie/Girl Scout troops may be interested in attending the event. Advance publicity could be posted on church bulletin boards, in children's specialty stores (i.e. clothing, shoes, toys) or through announcements and posters distributed around the community, since this is an excellent opportunity for mingling between the generations.

As a follow-up activity, some participants may be able to learn simple doll repair techniques and can form a group to fix broken and discarded dolls that can then be donated to needy children.

ENTERTAINERS

Professional entertainers may be willing to donate their time and talents at a geriatric facility. Such entertainers may include:

- Singers
- Dancers
- Ventriloquists

- Magicians
- Clowns
- Caricature Artists
- Comedians
- Musicians
- Impersonators of Famous People

Publicity is appreciated by any entertainer. Newspaper coverage is ideal and often quite easy to obtain, since most local newspapers are interested in obtaining photographs of human interest events to use as fillers.

EXERCISE AND PHYSICAL FITNESS PROGRAMS

Exercise plays an important role in physical fitness at any age. Physicians, therapists, and gerontologists all acknowledge the need for exercise in the later years. Exercise can result in such benefits as:

- Improved Cardiovascular Functioning
- Improved Muscle Tone
- Increased Strength
- Increased Endurance
- Improved Digestion
- Decreased Depression
- Decreased Confusion
- Improved Self-Esteem

A representative from a health spa or fitness club may be willing to lead an exercise group at the geriatric facility. It is important that the leader have some knowledge of the capacities and limitations of the participants; an exercise/fitness program for an active, healthy twenty year old is significantly different from that for an eighty year old, wheelchair-bound individual. Ideally, the program's nurse, occupational therapist, or physical therapist could collaborate with the exercise instructor to formulate a physiologically sound program that is relevant for geriatric populations.

Elderly members of the community (who are not usually

involved in the geriatric program) could be invited to participate in the exercise session. Appropriate means of contacting these individuals includes:

- Letting physicians know about the exercise group so that they could pass this information on to their patients.
- Posting information on bulletin boards in retirement homes or apartment complexes with large numbers of older people.
- Using bulletin boards in churches, grocery stores, and other places in the community.
- Contacting the newspaper for publicity of the event.

Exercise groups need to be held on a regular basis in order for maximum benefits to be achieved. If a professional exercise instructor is not available, a staff person or an able group member may lead the group.

TIP: Each participant's personal physician should be contacted prior to enrollment in the exercise sessions. It is crucial that group leaders be aware of any restrictions or contraindications.

FLORISTS
FLORAL DESIGNERS
FLOWER ARRANGING INSTRUCTION

Flowers can lift anyone's spirits and enliven any room. Florists might be willing to donate flowers which are still attractive but not quite fresh enough to sell. He or she might also be willing to provide instruction in the art of flower arranging. Silk flowers might also be used.

Family members might be invited to this event. The general public might also be interested in learning floral arranging. Posters could be displayed at the florist's shop and on community bulletin boards. Members of garden clubs might also wish to attend. Newspapers might be interested in printing notices of the upcoming event or actually covering the event with photos and text.

A floral arranging group could be held on a regular basis.

GREENHOUSES
NURSERIES
PLANT STORES

Caring for plants has been found to be very therapeutic for all age groups; in fact, the entire field of horticultural therapy is devoted just to this aspect. The manager or owner of a greenhouse, nursery, or plant store may be willing to bring a variety of plants to the geriatric facility and explain how to take care of each type.

Family members could be invited, as could the members of a garden club. Signs could be posted at plant stores and on community bulletin boards to inform the general public of this event.

The geriatric facility may wish to purchase a number of plants so that interested participants could care for them on a regular basis.

HANDWRITING ANALYSTS

Graphology is a fascinating science. People love to hear about what their handwriting reveals about their personality. A handwriting expert may be willing to come to the program and analyze handwriting samples of the participants. It can be a great deal of fun if the expert analyzes anonymous writing samples and the audience tries to guess who the writer was, on the basis of the discussed traits.

Family members might enjoy attending the event.

For follow-up, books on handwriting analysis could be made available.

HEALTH AGENCIES

Also listed under:

- Associations
- Clubs

• Social Service Organizations

Voluntary, nonprofit health agencies are usually able to send a speaker to talk before a large group. Possibilities include:

• American Arthritis Foundation
• American Cancer Society
• American Diabetes Association
• American Heart Association
• American Lung Association
• American Parkinson Disease Association
• Local and regional agencies serving the blind and deaf
• Mental Health Association

If some of these groups are not listed in the Yellow Pages, they can usually be found in the White Pages in alphabetical sequence.

The health agency might wish to publicize the event themselves so that interested members of the general public might attend.

Books for further information on health related topics should be made available.

HUMANE SOCIETIES

Many research studies have shown that pets bring therapeutic benefits to elderly persons. Humane societies are generally willing to bring several cats and dogs to visit the geriatric facility. All animals are carefully screened for their gentleness and good disposition. Participants are allowed to spend time with the animals, playing with or just holding them.

To ensure that each participant has as much time as possible with the animals, this event should be confined to a small group. Outside participation does not need to be solicited.

If the administrator of the facility permits, participants may wish to permanently adopt a pet for the facility.

KARATE AND OTHER MARTIAL ARTS INSTRUCTION

Karate, judo, and other martial arts techniques can be interesting to watch. Students and instructors from martial arts schools may be willing to demonstrate their skills at the geriatric facility.

If possible, newspaper coverage of the event will be appreciated by the martial arts instructor. Advertising the event around the community might be appropriate, since some members of the community might be interested in attending.

Similar events may be held on an occasional basis.

MAGICIANS
and
MAGICIANS' SUPPLIES

People of all ages are interested in magic. A magician might be found in the Yellow Pages or by contacting a magic supply store where the salespeople might be familiar with some of their customers who dabble in magic and might be willing to perform at the geriatric facility. In addition to performing, the magician might be willing to teach the audience simple magic tricks which could later be used to entertain their grandchildren or visiting youngsters.

The children of staff members and the grandchildren of participants might be invited to this event, as might local schoolchildren.

For follow-up, a staff member might obtain some books on magic and offer instruction to those individuals who are interested in learning magic.

MANICURES

A professional manicure makes anyone look well-groomed and consequently enhances self-esteem. Manicurists may be willing to come to the geriatric facility to demonstrate nail care. While some of the audience might actually receive a complete manicure, it will not be possible for *every* member of the audience to be manicured since the manicurist will not, in all likelihood, be able to devote the length of time it would require to do all participants.

This is best as a relatively small group activity, so outside participation does not need to be solicited.

A grooming group may be held on a regular basis. Participants may manicure their own nails or could give a manicure to another group member.

TIP: A registered nurse might need to determine each participant's appropriateness for inclusion in these sessions. Certain skin conditions or metabolic diseases might contraindicate participation in the group.

MODELING SCHOOLS

Schools which teach modeling may be delighted to send their students to the geriatric facility for a fashion show, since this would give the students a chance to model before a live audience.

Another possibility is for the students to instruct the geriatric participants in grooming and fashion techniques. It can also be fun to have the students teach the geriatric participants how to model and actually hold a fashion show.

Family members could be invited to this event, particularly if their relative is one of the models.

Grooming groups may be held on a regular basis as follow-up activities.

MUSEUMS

Art or historical museums may be willing to send an employee to the geriatric program for a lecture and exhibit.

Naturally, the most delicate or valuable items will not be able to be brought to the facility, but a lecture/exhibit with some representative artifacts or works of art may enable participants to experience the museum without leaving the facility.

Schoolchildren might be invited to attend the event.

Books on related topics should be made available to interested participants.

MUSIC INSTRUCTION—INSTRUMENTAL
MUSIC INSTRUCTION—VOCAL
and
MUSIC INSTRUMENTS—DEALERS

Music instructors might allow some of their students to perform at the geriatric facility. Music instrument dealers may also know of musicians who might be willing to perform.

The types of instruments might include:

- Accordion
- Clarinet
- Drums
- Flute
- Guitar
- Piano
- Saxophone
- Trumpet
- Violin
- Voice

The type of music could include any of the following:

- Classic
- Folk
- Gospel
- Jazz
- Opera
- Pop

- Rock
- Soul

The public might be invited to this event. Posters could be displayed at record and music stories in addition to other places around the community. Newspapers might also be willing to publicize the event

A possibility for follow-up activities is for interested individuals to receive music lessons from the students or teachers.

NURSES

Also listed under:

- Health Agencies
- Home Health Agencies
- Hospitals

Nursing agencies may agree to allow a registered nurse to come to the geriatric facility and lecture on topics of interest to older people. Relevant topics might include:

- Principles of Good Nutrition
- Exercise
- Diabetic Care
- Monitoring Heart Conditions
- Proper Taking of Medications

Older members of the community (who are not involved in the geriatric program) may wish to attend. Posters can be placed in physicians' offices, community bulletin boards, and in pharmacies.

A reading library of relevant topics on health should be made available for further reading.

OPTICAL GOODS—RETAIL

Since so many older people wear glasses, the manager or owner of an optical goods store might be willing to bring a large variety of eyeglass frames to the facility. Participants, many of whom have worn the same glasses or frames for years and years, might enjoy trying on new frames to see how they would look. The change that a new pair of glasses can make in someone's appearance is truly remarkable!

To ensure that participants all have a chance to try on the different pairs of glasses, outside participation should be minimal.

Participants may wish (but should be under no obligation) to have their lenses put into new frames or have new glasses made by the optician. The glasses, when ready, could be picked up at the store by a staff person.

ORCHID GROWERS

Most people are fascinated with orchids because of their infinite variety and beauty. An orchid grower might be willing to bring some orchids to the geriatric facility for a show. The lecture could include salient points on caring for orchids.

A local garden club might be invited to attend the event, as might the general public, by such means as newspaper publicity, posters in plant stores and greenhouses, and community bulletin boards.

As follow-up, interested participants may wish to form an orchid-growing group, purchasing and taking care of some of the more hardy and easily grown varieties.

PET SHOPS

Pet stores may be willing to bring a variety of animals to the geriatric program for a unique presentation. In addition to cats and dogs, watching and learning about exotic birds, fish, reptiles, and small animals can be fascinating.

The children of staff members and the grandchildren of

the participants might be invited to this event.

The participants may wish to get a pet for the facility on a permanent basis. Tropical fish, cats, dogs, or birds might be appropriate.

PHYSICIANS AND SURGEONS—MD

Also listed under:

- Chiropractors
- Optometrists
- Physicians and Surgeons—DO (Osteopaths)
- Physicians and Surgeons—DPM (Podiatrists)

Physicians may be willing to lecture on their areas of expertise. Possible specialties include:

- Family practice or internal medicine
  General principles of good health, nutrition, exercise.
- Ailments and diseases common to the elderly, including prevention and treatment.
- Cardiology
  Heart problems and their treatment.
- Neurology
  Prevention and treatment of strokes and other neurological diseases.
- Dermatology
  Skin care for the older person; skin problems and their treatment.
- Gastroenterology
  Treatment of digestive system problems.
- Opthamology
  The treatment of changes and diseases of the eyes brought about by aging.
- Gynecology
  Problems experienced by older women.
- Otolaryngology
  Problems with the ears due to aging.

- Psychiatry
  Principles of good mental health; diagnosis and treatment of psychiatric problems experienced by the elderly.
- Pulmonary
  Respiratory diseases experienced by the elderly.
- Rheumatology
  Coping with arthritis.
- Urology
  Prostate problems common to older men.
- Podiatry
  Proper foot care, including the selection of shoes; problems such as bunions, corns, calluses, ingrown nails, fungus.
- Optometry
  Geriatric optometry, including diagnosis and treatment of visual problems in the elderly.

The physician may wish to post a sign in his or her office to inform patients of the upcoming lecture. Older members of the community should be invited. The lecture could be advertised in the newspaper and on bulletin boards around the community.

For follow-up, books for further reading on the various topics should be made available.

SCHOOLS

Many research studies have revealed the positive effects of interaction between youngsters and elderly individuals. Both generations can benefit from exposure to and interaction with each other. Schools, whether public or private, preschool or secondary, are probably *the* best resource for locating and involving youngsters in the geriatric programs. A good relationship with a local school can result in many meaningful experiences for both the students and the geriatric participants.

Listed below are just a few of the many possibilities for utilizing schools in geriatric programs.

Preschools

- A regularly scheduled "Adopt a Grandparent" program in which preschool children visit with their assigned "grandparent" for a certain length of time (generally about thirty minutes).
  To assure continuity and close relationships, this visitation program ideally takes place on a weekly basis.
- Special performances by the youngsters.
  This may include holiday music programs, short skits, or "show and tell" sessions in which the youngsters bring a favorite pet, object, or their own artwork to present and discuss.
- Participation in events sponsored by the geriatric program.
  For example, the geriatric participants might sponsor an Easter egg hunt in which they hide eggs before the youngsters arrive.

Elementary and Middle Schools

(Private schools generally appear under this listing, while public schools may not. To locate the addresses/phone numbers of public schools, it may be necessary to use the White Pages and locate the listing under the section on the specific town or county. Schools usually appear in this section under the listings of Schools, Board of Education, or *Public Education*.)

- A regularly scheduled "Adopt a Grandparent" program in which the students visit with their assigned "grandparent" for a certain length of time (about an hour). To assure continuity and close relationships, this visitation program ideally takes place at least two to four times a month.
- In-between visitations or perhaps in lieu of visitations, an ongoing pen pal program might be beneficial for both generations. Teachers may find such a project to be an excellent means of practicing handwriting and English skills.

- Special performances by the youngsters are always enjoyable. Under this category fall such things as:
  - plays
  - acrobatics
  - music recitals
  - dance recitals
  - show-and-tell presentations
  - holiday projects and presentations (i.e. a costume parade at Halloween)
  - class projects and reports in which the students have to interview an older person to find out such information as what the person did for recreation as a child; what the area was like fifty years earlier; customs, foods, holidays from the country or geographic region in which the older person was born.

Middle and High Schools

- A regularly scheduled "Adopt a Grandparent" program in which the students visit with their assigned "grandparent." This visitation program ideally takes place at least two to four times a month.
- In-between visitations or in lieu of visitations, an ongoing pen pal program between the students and elderly persons.
- Special performances such as plays, dance, and music recitals.
- Participation in events sponsored by the geriatric program:
  - Geography/history/social studies classes might be interested in attending special foreign days to learn more about different cultures.
  - Foreign language classes might also be interested in attending special foreign days. For example, a German class might perform German songs and dances for an Oktoberfest celebration.
  - Home economics classes might be willing to sponsor a party at the geriatric facility, complete with party food made by the class.

- Health or physical education classes might be interested in leading an exercise group *under supervision of the program's physical therapist or nurse* to ensure that exercises are appropriate and not overly strenuous.
- Art classes might present a show of their work or could paint a mural at the facility.
- Psychology, sociology, or health occupations classes might be interested in field trips to the facility to learn more about gerontology.
- Service clubs might get involved in volunteer work after school.

Colleges and Universities

(In lieu of or in addition to listings in the Yellow Pages, colleges and universities might be found in the White Pages, listed alphabetically or under the county/state in which it is located if a public two- or four-year college or university.)

- Health classes (under the Physical Education Department) or health education classes (under the Education Department) might present a lecture or series of lectures on nutrition, exercise, safety, and other aspects of good health.
- Dance classes (under the Departments of Dance, Theater, or Physical Education) might be interested in performing at the facility or in involving the geriatric participants in a dance therapy session.
- Nursing and medical students might spend time at the geriatric program in order to learn more about gerontology.
- Many colleges are beginning gerontology programs. Students from such classes have an avid interest in the elderly and might wish to be involved in a geriatric program.
- Nutrition or home economics students might lecture on nutrition.
- Pharmacy students could lecture on the correct use of medications.
- Physical therapy students might lead exercise classes.

- Occupational therapy students could lead sensory integration groups, remotivation classes, or therapeutic activity sessions.
- Recreation students could lead therapeutic recreation sessions.
- Psychology students might lead reality orientation or remotivation groups.
- Social work and counseling students may be involved in counseling sessions with the geriatric participants and/or their families.
- Poetry students might read their poems or involve the participants in creating their own.
- Art students may be involved in the ways delineated under the section of "Art Instruction and Schools" in this chapter.
- Theater or music students may perform at the facility.
- Education students might teach an adult class or current events, basic adult education, or special interests.
- Accounting students may wish to volunteer their services for the preparation of income tax returns.
- Law students may be willing to volunteer their services to help solve simple legal problems.

Special Schools

Schools which offer specialized instruction might be listed in the Yellow Pages. They may be utilized in various ways, many of which are discussed in their respective sections in this chapter.

- Beauty schools ... see "Barbers, Beauty Salons, and Beauty Schools."
- Paraprofessional medical training ... nursing aide students may assist the elderly as needed or simply visit with them.
- Schools of dance ... see "Dancing Instruction."
- Music schools ... see "Music Instruction."
- Acting schools ... students may perform at the facility.

• Art schools...see "Art Instruction and Schools."
• Modeling schools...see "Modeling Schools."

SPORTSWEAR—RETAIL AND WHOLESALE
MEN'S CLOTHING
WOMEN'S APPAREL

Managers and owners of clothing stores and manufacturing firms might be willing to sponsor fashion shows at the geriatric facility. The clothes might be modelled by professional models or by the store's employees, staff members, or the geriatric participants.

It may be appropriate to arrange for the clothes and accessories to be offered for sale after the fashion show, provided that members of the audience do not feel under obligation or pressure to buy.

Advance publicity for this event should be posted around the facility so that family members can attend, as well as around the community (i.e. at the sponsoring store, drug and grocery stores, and other public places). Newspaper coverage of the event may also be a possibility.

Since styles and merchandise change rapidly, fashion shows may be held several times throughout the year.

SQUARE DANCE APPAREL
SQUARE DANCE CALLERS
WESTERN APPAREL
WESTERN WEAR

Square dancing is enjoyable for both the observers and participants. Many of the dances can be easily learned, especially since most involve a partner who can guide the inexperienced participant. Even wheelchair-bound individuals can participate in many of the dances.

Arranging for square dancers to perform at the geriatric facility is seldom a problem. Most square dancers are more than willing to dance in front of an audience and even to directly involve the audience. A square dance caller will undoubtedly know of a square dance group, as will stores which sell square dance apparel. Stores which sell Western clothing are another possibility.

Family members of all ages could be invited to attend this fun event.

As follow-up activities, square dancing groups could be held on a regular basis.

STAMPS FOR COLLECTORS

Many people enjoy looking at and collecting postage stamps from foreign countries or from different periods of time. A lecture and exhibit of some of the most unique stamps can be quite educational in addition to being entertaining. Many of the stamps are aesthetically very pleasing. Individuals who work in stamp stores are usually very knowledgeable about stamps and might be willing to bring a variety of them to the geriatric facility. These stamp dealers might also know of individual stamp collectors who collect stamps of special relevance to a specific population (i.e. stamps from Ireland if a large proportion of the participants are Irish) and who might enjoy discussing their collections.

History or geography classes from a nearby school might be invited to attend the lecture.

For follow-up, books on stamp collecting should be made available to interested readers. A stamp collecting group could meet on a regular basis.

TRAVEL AGENCIES

Travelogues are popular with people of all ages. Such "armchair travel" gives geriatric populations a chance to see different sights and to re-experience past travel. Travel agents may have a collection of slides and movies from a variety of trips or may know of some clients who have taken interesting trips. Most travelers are very willing to discuss their trips and present slides to an audience!

Such travelogues could stand as an event on their own or could be incorporated as part of a special foreign day (i.e. a film on China as part of a Chinese New Year's celebration).

Family members could be invited to this event, as could the general public. Posters might be placed on bulletin boards in libraries and churches. Social studies classes from nearby schools might wish to attend.

Books on each country might be made available to interested readers. A continuing travel series might be held on a regular basis.

Chapter 5

PUBLIC LIBRARIES

The local public library is another means of learning about and locating resources within the community. Cultivating a good relationship with the reference librarian can result in new possibilities for the geriatric program. There are several ways to utilize the public library for information.

Almost all libraries have a bulletin board on which various notices are posted. This can be a good way to obtain names and phone numbers of people or clubs who might be interested in sharing their expertise, talents, or interests with the participants of the geriatric program. Possibilities include:

- Civic and social service groups.
  Such groups might be willing to volunteer to help with a special project at the facility or simply to visit participants on a regular basis.
- Health organizations.
  Such groups could sponsor lectures on health-related topics.
- Hobby or other special interest groups.
  Such groups might include clubs for stamp collecting, oil painting, foreign languages, orchid growing, gourmet cooking, and many others. Group members may be willing

to provide exhibits, lectures, demonstrations, or instructions.

- Entertainers.
Singers, musicians, magicians, dancers, and others might be primarily interested in securing paid engagements, but might be willing to entertain for a nominal fee or on a no-fee basis at the geriatric facility.

Most libraries sponsor lectures, travelogues, entertainment, and meetings of individuals and clubs with educational or cultural aspects. Notification of these events is posted at the sponsoring library and, usually, in the local newspapers. The names and phone numbers of the contact person for each event can be obtained from a library employee.

The reference department may have pamphlets or booklets which list such community resources as:

- Civic and Social Service Groups
- Health Organizations
- Hobby or Other Special Interest Groups
- Entertainers
- Professional Organizations
- Social Fraternities and Sororities (i.e. Elks, Moose, Shriners)
- Religious/Ethnic/Social Service Organizations (such as Catholic Youth Organization or B'nai Brith)

Almost without exception, reference departments in public libraries all own copies of the *Encyclopedia of Associations* published by Gale Research Company. This is a most helpful tool for obtaining community resources. Updated each year, the *Encyclopedia of Associations* lists virtually every association in the United States. Categories which are pertinent to geriatric populations include:

- Athletic and Sport Organizations
- Cultural Organizations
- Educational Organizations
- Fraternal, Foreign Interest, Nationality, and Ethnic Organizations

- Health and Medical Organizations
- Hobby and Avocational Organizations
- Public Affairs Organizations
- Religious Organizations
- Social Welfare Organizations
- Veteran, Hereditary, and Patriotic Organizations

Each listing contains the name of the contact person, address, phone number, number of members, and a brief description of the purpose of scope of the organization.

The reader who is searching for resources for his or her program should keep in mind that each association has members and chapters located all over the country. The address of the national headquarters or contact person may be in a distant state, but there may well be a local chapter or member in the very same (or nearby) city as the geriatric program. For example, the Society for Creative Anachronism, a group which provides exhibits and demonstrations of medieval life, is headquartered in Milpitas, California, but has 500 local groups throughout the country. Chances are good that there might be a few members in a geographically accessible city. Chances are even better for locating a local member of the National Association for Widowed People because this group, although headed by a resident of Springfield, Illinois, has 3,000 local chapters all throughout the country. Altrusa International, a women's service club, is headquartered in Chicago, but membership is definitely not confined to that city, since there are 580 local groups.

Since there may be a local chapter of an organization which could get involved with the geriatric program, it behooves the activity planner to write to the national contact person of each association which sounds promising. There is nothing to lose by trying (except the cost of postage), and everything to be gained (namely, a new community resource). Since many of these associations are not listed in the local phone book, this is frequently the only way to learn about and contact these associations.

Because many of the associations function on a very tight budget, enclosing a stamped, self-addressed envelope is always appreciated.

The following pages, based on the *Encyclopedia of Associations,* list some associations which might be of interest to geriatric programs. Because the actual *Encyclopedia of Associations* has many, many more listings, the reader is urged to consult this two-volume encyclopedia.

Chapter 6

ASSOCIATIONS AND SOCIETIES

Associations devoted to the study and advocacy of aging individuals may be willing to provide experts in the field of gerontology who can lecture on geriatric problems and their solutions

American Association of Retired Persons
1909 K Street, N.W.
Washington, D.C. 20049

Center for the Study of Aging
706 Madison Avenue
Albany, New York 12208

Institute for Retired Professionals
New School for Social Research
66 West 12th Street
New York, New York 10011

National Association of Mature People
Box 26792
Oklahoma City, Oklahoma 73126

National Council of Senior Citizens
925 25th Street, N.W.
Washington, D.C. 20005

National Council on Aging
600 Maryland Avenue, S.W.
West Wing 100, Suite 208
Washington, D.C. 20024

National Interfaith Coalition on Aging
P.O. Box 1924
298 Hull Street
Athens, Georgia 30603

ETHNIC AND INTERNATIONAL ASSOCIATIONS

Various ethnic and international groups might be willing to come to geriatric facilities to entertain. Possibilities include native music, folk dancing, ethnic foods, and travelogues-lectures.

Africa Guild
163 West 23rd Street
New York, New York 10011

Africa Heritage Center for African Dance and Music
420 Seventh Street, N.W.
Washington, D.C. 20004

Afro-American Cultural Foundation
P.O. Box 587
White Plains, New York 10602

America-Italy Society
667 Madison Avenue
New York, New York 10021

American Council of Polish American Clubs
c/o Stanley A. Ciesielski
610 Windwood Road
Baltimore, Maryland 21212

American Jewish Historical Society
Two Thornton Road
Waltham, Massachusetts 02154

American Portuguese Society
Professional Building
555 Lake Avenue
Saint James, New York 11780

American Scandinavian Foundation
127 East 73rd Street
New York, New York 10021

American Siam Society
633 24th Street
Santa Monica, California 90402

Armenian Assembly Charitable Trust
1420 N Street, N.W.
Washington, D.C. 20005

Assemblee Des Franco-Americans/
Association of Franco-Americans
P.O. Box 2094
Union, New Jersey 07083
    Comments: French culture.

Asia Society
725 Park Avenue
New York, New York 10021

Association of Hispanic Arts
200 East 87th Street
New York, New York 10028

Association of Student and Professional
    Italian-Americans
P.O. Box 3672, Grand Central Station
New York, New York, 10017

Austrian Forum
11 East 52nd Street
New York, New York 10022

Caribbean-American Intercultural Organization
1629 Columbia Road, N.W.
Suite 114
Washington, D.C. 20009

Center for Arab-Islamic Studies
P.O. Box 543
Brattleboro, Vermont 05301

Chinese Culture Association
P.O. Box 1272
Palo Alto, California 94302

Czechoslavak Society of Arts and Sciences
2067 Park Road, N.W.
Washington, D.C. 20010

Federation of Alpine and Schuhplattler Clubs
    in North America
54 Cathedral Lane
Cheektowaga, New York 14225
    Comments: Bavarian and Austrian culture and dance.

Foundation for Ethnic Dance
17 West 71st Street
New York, New York 10023
    Comments: Ethnic dance of all types.

Hajji Baba Club
c/o Jeanette Longyear Smith
301 East 47th Street
New York, New York 10017
    Comments: Collectors of Islamic art and Oriental rugs.

Irish American Cultural Association
10415 South Western
Chicago, Illinois 60643

Japan Society
333 East 47th Street
New York, New York 10017

Norwegian American Historical Association
Saint Olaf College
Northfield, Minnesota 55057

Panamerican Cultural Circle
16 Malvern Place
Verona, New Jersey 07044

Society for German-American Studies
c/o Don Heinrich Tolzmann
3418 Boudinot Avenue
Cincinnati, Ohio 45211

Swiss-American Historical Society
c/o Marianne Burkhard
German Department
3072 Foreign Languages Building
707 South Mathews
University of Illinois
Urbana, Illinois 61801

Ukrainian Institute of America
Two East 79th Street
New York, New York 10021

HEALTH AND MEDICAL ORGANIZATIONS

Organizations dedicated to promoting health may be able to provide informative lectures at a geriatric facility or to participate in other projects.

American Diabetes Association
Two Park Place
New York, New York 10016
    Comments: For diabetics.

American Foundation for the Blind
15 West 16th Street
New York, New York 10011
    Comments: Clearinghouse for local and regional agencies serving the blind.

American Geriatrics Society
· Ten Columbus Circle
New York, New York, 10019
  Comments: For physicians interested in geriatrics.

American Heart Association
7320 Greenville Avenue
Dallas, Texas 75231
  Comments: Heart and circulatory disease.

American Holistic Medical Association
6932 Little River Turnpike
Annandale, Virginia 22003
  Comments: For doctors of medicine and osteopathy
             who are interested in holistic treatment.

Depressives Anonymous
P.O. Box 1777, Grand Central Station
New York, New York 10017
  Comments: Deals with anxiety and depression.

Emotional Health Anonymous
2420 San Gabriel Boulevard
Rosemead, California 91770
  Comments: Promotes psychological good health.

Gerontological Society of America
1835 K Street, N.W.
Suite 305
Washington, D.C. 20006
  Comments: For professionals who are interested in the
             scientific study of aging. Includes physi-
             cians, psychologists, pharmacologists, psy-
             chiatrists, physiologists, biochemists, and
             sociologists.

Laughter Therapy
P.O. Box 827
· Monterey, California 93940
  Comments: Supplies tapes of the *Candid Camera* tele-
             vision comedy shows to nursing homes,
             hospitals, and other health facilities.

Mended Hearts
7320 Greenville Avenue
Dallas, Texas 75231
    Comments: For patients who have undergone heart sur-
        gery.

National Association of the Deaf
814 Thayer Avenue
Silver Spring, Maryland 20910
    Comments: For hearing impaired individuals.

National Center for Homeopathy
1500 Massachusetts Avenue, N.W.
Suite 41
Washington, D.C. 20005
    Comments: Has a speaker's bureau for lectures on nat-
        ural healing.

National Council for Therapy and Rehabilitation
    through Horticulture
701 North Saint Aspah Street
Alexandria, Virginia 22314
    Comments: Interested in garden clubs and other horti-
        cultural ventures for geriatric populations.

National Council on Wholistic Therapeutics
    and Medicine
271 Fifth Avenue
Suite 3
New York, New York 10016
    Comments: Preventive medicine.

National Herbalist Association
271 Fifth Avenue
Suite 3
New York, New York 10016
    Comments: Has a speaker's bureau. Concerned with
        healing qualities of plants.

Therapy Dogs International
1536 Morris Place
Hillside, New Jersey 07205
  Comments: Provides formal obedience training for dogs
             of various breeds with good temperaments
             who can live in nursing homes and provide
             companionship.

Touch for Health Foundation
1174 North Lake Avenue
Pasadena, California 91104
  Comments: Composed of physicians, chiropractors,
             physical therapists, massage therapists, and
             others who are interested in the therapeutic
             potential of massage.

MUSIC ASSOCIATIONS

Members of music associations may be willing to come
to the geriatric facility and entertain. In some cases, musicians may even be willing to teach the geriatric participants
how to play some of the musical instruments.

Amateur Chamber Music Players
633 E Street, N.W.
Washington, D.C. 20004

Amateur Organist Association International
7720 Morgan Avenue, South
Minneapolis, Minnesota 55423

American Accordionists' Association
580 Kearny Avenue
Kearny, New Jersey 07032

American Banjo Fraternity
2665 Woodstock Road
Columbus, Ohio 43221

American Guild of English Handbell Ringers
601 West Riverview Drive
Dayton, Ohio 45406

American Harp Society
6331 Quebec Drive
Hollywood California 90068

American Recorder Society
48 West 21st Street
New York, New York 10010

American Society for Jewish Music
155 Fifth Avenue
New York, New York 10010
    Comments: Secular, folk, old, new, and liturgical music.

American Union of Swedish Singers
c/o Martin Ahlm
Nelson World Travel Bureau
333 North Michigan Avenue
Chicago, Illinois 60601

American Viola Society
512 Roosevelt Boulevard
Ypsilanti, Michigan 48197

Black Music Association
1500 Locust
Suite 1905
Philadelphia, Pennsylvania 19102

Chinese Music Society of North America
2329 Charmingfare
Woodridge, Illinois 60517

Polish Singers Alliance of America
1217 78th Street
Brooklyn, New York 11228

Society for the Preservation and Advancement
of the Harmonicas
P.O. Box 865
Troy, Michigan 48099

Society for the Preservation and Encouragement
of Barber Shop Quartet Singing in America
P.O. Box 575
6315 Third Avenue
Kenosha, Wisconsin 53141

Sweet Adelines
P.O. Box 45168
Tulsa, Oklahoma 74147
Comments: Women's barbershop harmony singing.

SERVICE ORGANIZATIONS

Many organizations are service-oriented, devoted to helping other people in a variety of ways. Some of these organizations are nationally based, but have local chapters which might be interested in a local project with a geriatric population. Involvement could be through such means as:

• Once a year holiday or other kind of entertainment.
• Regularly scheduled one-on-one visitations on a weekly or monthly basis.
• Donations of money or material items.

Altrusa International
Eight South Michigan Avenue
Chicago, Illinois 60603
Comments: An executive and professional women's group that helps with community civic and social welfare problems.

Association of Junior Leagues
825 Third Avenue
New York, New York 10022
Comments: A group for women from eighteen to forty-five years of age.

Boys Clubs of America
771 First Avenue
New York, New York 10017
　Comments: To promote character development of youth.

Boy Scouts of America
1325 Walnut Hill Lane
Irving, Texas 75062
　Comments: For boys and young men.

Bread and Roses
78 Throckmorton Avenue
Mill Valley, California 94941
　Comments: Volunteer entertainers who bring free, live
　　　　　　 entertainment to nursing homes. Has a
　　　　　　 handbook on how to develop similar orga-
　　　　　　 nizations.

Circle K International
3636 Woodview Trace
Indianapolis, Indiana 46268
　Comments: A group of college students to serve campus
　　　　　　 and community.

Civitan International
P.O. Box 2102
Birmingham, Alabama 35201
　Comments: For business and professional men and
　　　　　　 women. Stresses good citizenship on local,
　　　　　　 national, and international levels, includ-
　　　　　　 ing aid to physically and mentally handi-
　　　　　　 capped individuals.

Girls Clubs of America
205 Lexington Avenue
New York, New York 10016
　Comments: For girls.

Girl Scouts of America
830 Third Avenue and 51st Street
New York, New York 10022
　Comments: For girls and young women.

Good Bears of the World
Box 8236
Honolulu, Hawaii 96815
    Comments: Promotes, collects, and distributes teddy
            bears to children in hospitals and senior
            citizens in institutions. Since approximately
            half of all Americans grew up owning a
            teddy bear, this group claims that teddy
            bears can be a source of comfort to old and
            young people alike.

Hospital Audiences, Incorporated
1540 Broadway
New York, New York 10036
    Comments: Promotes cultural enrichment of elderly
            and disabled individuals in nursing homes,
            hospitals, and other institutions.

Jaycees International
P.O. Box 40577
Coral Gables, Florida 33134
    Comments: An organization for young men (eighteen
            to forty years old) who are interested in
            community development projects.

Junior Optimist Clubs
4494 Lindell Boulevard
Saint Louis, Missouri 63108
    Comments: For boys and girls in grades six to nine.

Key Club International
3636 Woodview Trace
Indianapolis, Indiana 46268
    Comments: Sponsored by Kiwanis for high school stu-
            dents interested in serving others.

Kiwanis International
3636 Woodview Trace
Indianapolis, Indiana 46268
    Comments: Business and professional men's civic serv-
            ice club.

Ki-Wives International
c/o Nita Bradley
R.D. #1, Box 102
Delmar, Delaware 19940
   Comments: Wives of Kiwanis members.

Lions (and Lioness) Club International
300 22nd Street
Oak Brook, Illinois 60570
   Comments: A business and professional men's (and
      women's) community service club.

Make Today Count
P.O. Box 303
Burlington, Iowa 52601
   Comments: For cancer patients and their immediate
      families, as well as terminally ill victims of
      other incurable diseases. Helps to lessen
      emotional trauma.

National Assistance League
5627 Fernwood Avenue
Los Angeles, California 90028
   Comments: Projects often include geriatric programs
      (i.e. acting as a friend to a person in need).

National Association for Widowed People
P.O. Box 3564
Springfield, Illinois 62708
   Comments: Local chapters offer support for widowed
      people.

National Association of Extension Home Economists
c/o Deloris J. Ellis
315 North 6th Street
DeKalb, Illinois 60115
   Comments: Offers out-of-school educational programs
      of nutrition, energy conservation, and bud-
      geting.

National Association of Junior Auxiliaries
P.O. Box 1873
Greenville, Mississippi 38701
Comments: A young women's group.

National Association of Negro Business and
Professional Women's Clubs
1806 New Hampshire Avenue, N.W.
Washington, D.C. 20009
Comments: Encourages freedom, dignity, self-respect,
and self-reliance.

National Shut-In Society
225 West 99th Street
New York, New York 10025
Comments: Gives cheer and comfort to chronic invalids.

Pilot Club International
P.O. Box 4844
244 College Street
Macon, Georgia 31213
Comments: A civic service group for executive and pro-
fessional women.

Quota International
1828 L Street, N.W.
Washington, D.C. 20036
Comments: A civic service group for executive and professional women.

Rotary International
1600 Ridge Avenue
Evanston, Illinois 60201
Comments: For business and professional executives.

Ruritan National
Dublin, Virginia 24084
Comments: A civic service group for towns with popu-
lations under 5,000 people.

Sertoma International
1912 East Meyer Boulevard
Kansas City, Missouri 64132
    Comments: A business and professional men's group
              interested in hearing and speech disorders.

The Fish
c/o Anchor Society
2398 Pine Street
San Francisco, California 94115
    Comments: May serve in such projects as reading to the
              blind, preparing meals, and running errands
              for the elderly.

Uncap International
2613 Huron Street
Los Angeles, California 90065
    Comments: Helps the handicapped to become involved
              in hobbies.

US Jayceettes
Box 7
Tulsa, Oklahoma 74121
    Comments: An organization for young women (eigh-
              teen to forty years old) who are interested in
              community development projects.

We Can Do!
P.O. Box 723
Arcadia, California 91006
    Comments: Offers help for cancer patients. Does not
              offer medical advice, but emphasizes self-
              help through biofeedback, laughter, and
              relaxation.

Widowed Persons Service
1909 K Street, N.W.
Washington, D.C. 20049
    Comments: A program of the American Association of
              Retired Persons (AARP). Volunteers (who

have been widowed at least two years) offer
support to new widows and widowers.

SPECIAL INTEREST ASSOCIATIONS

There is an infinite variety of associations which serve
special needs and interests. Only a small percentage of
hobby and avocational associations are listed here. The
Encyclopedia of Associations offers many more listings
which are not included in this book. Such associations
range from those dedicated to a single flower or plant (such
as orchids, African violets, daffodils, and cactus) to specific
games (such as backgammon, Go, Mah Jongg, Tiddlywinks,
and Scrabble); from those for specific breeds of dogs to
those which study a specific author (such as Charles Dickens,
Bernard Shaw, or Charlotte Bronte) to those for the study of
a composer (such as Duke Ellington or Richard Wagner).
Others are dedicated to extremely specialized fields such as
Egyptology.

Associations for collectors are numerous. Collectibles
may include such items as:

- Antique Valentines
- Autographs
- Beads
- Beer Cans
- Beer Steins
- Bottles
- Bottle-Openers
- Business Cards
- Buttons
- Cigarette Packs
- Citrus Labels
- Coca-Cola Memorabilia
- Corkscrews
- Folding Fans
- Hatpins

- Hubcaps
- Japanese Swords
- Knives
- Mickey Mouse Items
- Newspapers
- Olympic Pins
- Plates
- Thermometers
- Thimbles
- Wine Labels

Whatever an individual's hobby or special interest, chances are that other people also share it and have formed an association to pursue that interest.

American Cat Fanciers Association
P.O. Box 203
Point Lookout, Missouri 65726
   Comments: Could sponsor cat shows and bring cats for
      visits.

American Center of the Union Internationale
   De La Marionnette
Browning Road
Hyde Park, New York 12538
   Comments: Puppetry.

American Homebrewers Association
Box 287
Boulder, Colorado 80306
   Comments: Could give lectures and demonstrations on
      beer-making.

Antique Automobile Club of America
501 West Governor Road
Hershey, Pennsylvania 17033
   Comments: Members might be willing to exhibit their
      cars at the geriatric facility.

Bald-Headed Men of America
4006 Arendell Street
Morehead City, North Carolina 28557
> Comments: A whimsical group dedicated to the belief that "bald is beautiful." Gives speeches on self-esteem for bald-headed men. Publishes a newsletter called *Chrome-Dome*. Could help with a "Best Chrome Dome Contest."

Callerlab-International Association of Square
    Dance Callers
Pocono Pines, Pennsylvania 18350
> Comments: Could provide leads for square dance groups who are willing to entertain.

Chinese Snuff Bottle Society
2601 North Charles Street
Baltimore, Maryland 21218
> Comments: Members may be willing to exhibit bottles.

Clowns of America
P.O. Box 3906
Baltimore, Maryland 21222
> Comments: Professional and amateur clowns, magicians, puppeteers, and jugglers could entertain.

Doll Collectors of America
14 Chestnut Street
Westford, Massachusetts 01886
> Comments: Members may be willing to bring unique dolls to the geriatric facility for exhibits.

Gavel Clubs
2200 North Grand Avenue
Santa Ana, California 92711
> Comments: A public speaking group whose members might welcome an opportunity to speak in front of a group.

Hug Club
P.O. Box 453
Laguna Beach, California 92652
    Comments: Promotes hugging for its therapeutic bene-
             fits of stress reduction, diminished anger,
             and strengthened relationships. Members
             might provide lectures. Club offers a vari-
             ety of Hug Club paraphernelia.

International Brotherhood of Magicians
28 North Main Street
Kenton, Ohio 43326
    Comments: Magic shows.

International Graphoanalysis Society
111 North Canal Street
Chicago, Illinois 60606
    Comments: Members may be willing to come to the ger-
             iatric facility and demonstrate the science
             of handwriting analysis.

International Old Lacers
P.O. Box 1029
Westminster, Colorado 80030
    Comments: Members could exhibit their collections of
             antique laces.

International Society of Wine Tasters
60 Sheridan Avenue
Williston Park, New York 11596
    Comments: May sponsor a wine tasting seminar.

International Toastmistress Clubs
2519 Woodland Drive
Anaheim, California 92801
    Comments: A public speaking group (for women) whose
             members might welcome an opportunity
             to speak in front of a group.

Music Box Society, International
Box 205, Route 3
Morgantown, Indiana 46160

Comments: Members may be willing to exhibit their music boxes and musical figurines.

National Association of Miniature Enthusiasts
P.O. Box 2621
Anaheim, California 92804
Comments: Members might exhibit their collections of miniatures.

National Federation of State Poetry Societies
c/o Jack Murphy
1121 Major Avenue, N.W.
Albuquerque, New Mexico 87107
Comments: Poets may give readings of their own work or the work of others. They may also lead poetry therapy groups, encouraging participants to express themselves through poetry.

National Clogging and Hoedown Council
425 Poinsett Drive
Chapel Hill, North Carolina 27514
Comments: Could demonstrate clogging and other types of folk dancing.

National Council of State Garden Clubs
4401 Magnolia Avenue
Saint Louis, Missouri 63110
Comments: Members might exhibit plants and flowers at the geriatric facility. They could also help to establish a gardening/horticultural group at the facility.

National Safety Council
444 North Michigan Avenue
Chicago, Illinois 60611
Comments: Could provide lectures on safety.

Old Old Timers Club
c/o A. J. Gironda
Box AA
Mamaroneck, New York 10543

Comments: Enables men and women who have been in amateur radio communications for forty years or more to establish contact with each other.

Society for Creative Anachronism
P.O. Box 743
Milpitas, California 95035
Comments: This group researches the Middle Ages and provides exhibits and demonstrations of pre-1650 culture for schools and other groups. Tournaments are held to enable members to display their skills in medieval music, dancing, fighting, and creating artifacts such as costumes, armor, and embroidery. The group creates a total medieval environment in which everyone is a participant rather than a spectator.

Toastmasters International
P.O. Box 10400
2200 North Grand Avenue
Santa Ana, California 92711
Comments: A public speaking group (for men) whose members might welcome an opportunity to speak in front of a group.

United Federation of Doll Clubs
P.O. Box 14146
Eight B. East Street
Parkville, Missouri 64152
Comments: Members may be willing to bring unique dolls to the geriatric facility for exhibits.

Voicespondence Club
c/o Howard W. McClelland
Box 259
Trexlertown, Pennsylvania 18087
Comments: For blind and sighted people who have access to tape recorders. Members can exchange tapes of ideas, music, and conversation.

ASSOCIATIONS FOR THE VISUAL ARTS

A variety of associations promote and serve the fine and creative arts. Members of these groups may be willing to come to the geriatric facility to lecture or demonstrate their art.

Affiliate Artists
155 West 68th Street
Suite 35F
New York, New York 10023
   Comments: Sponsors residency programs where artists perform in informal community settings such as schools, churches, and factories.

American Watercolor Society
14 East 90th Street
New York, New York 1028

Caricaturists Society of America
218 West 47th Street
New York, New York 10036

Cartoonists Guild
156 West 72nd Street
New York, New York 10023

Center for the History of American Needlework
Old Economy Village
14th and Church Street
Ambridge, Pennsylvania 15003

Coalition of Women's Art Organizations
Box 3304, Grand Central Station
New York, New York 10017
   Comments: Maintains speaker's bureau; gives recognition to women artists.

Elder Craftsmen
135 East 65th Street
New York, New York 10021

Comments: A nonprofit outlet for older people to exhibit and sell their handwork on consign-
ment.

Federation of Modern Painters and Sculptors
c/o Haim Mendelson
234 West 21st Street
New York, New York 10011

Handweavers Guild of America
65 La Salle Road
West Hartford, Connecticut 06107
Comments: Emphasis on weaving and hand spinning.

International Center of Medieval Art
The Cloisters
Fort Tryon Park
New York, New York 10040
Comments: Promotes the study of medieval art and civ-
ilization between 325 and 1500 A.D.

International Guild of Candle Artisans
9428 Brush Run
Columbia, Maryland 21045

National Cartoonists Society
Nine Ebony Court
Brooklyn, New York 11229

National Center on Arts and the Aging
600 Maryland Avenue, S.W.
West Wing 100
Washington, D.C. 20024
Comments: This program (as a part of the National
Council on the Aging) tries to stimulate a
national awareness of the importance of
the arts to geriatric populations. Acts as a
national clearing house for program and
funding resources.

National Committee on Art Education for the Elderly
Culver Stockton College
Canton, Missouri 63435
> Comments: Promotes research and development of art
> education opportunities for geriatric popu-
> lations, helping to establish programs, ser-
> vices, and facilities.

National Council on Education for the Ceramic Arts
c/o Regina Brown
P.O. Box 1677
Bandon, Oregon 97411

National Watercolor Society
c/o Ruth Eyrich
2408 Daneland
Lakewood, California 90712

Pen and Brush Inc.
16 East Tenth Street
New York, New York 10003
> Comments: Professional women artists, sculptors, crafts-
> men, and musicians.

Performing and Visual Arts Society
P.O. Box 102
Kinnealon, New Jersey 07405
> Comments: Encourages creativity in high school juniors
> and seniors. Includes dance, drama, music,
> puppetry, graphic arts, industrial arts, fash-
> ion design, culinary arts, creative writing,
> and fine arts.

Society of Animal Artists
151 Carroll Street, City Island
Bronx, New York 10463
> Comments: Painting and sculpting of animals, birds,
> and fish.

Society of Batik Artists
c/o Astrith Deyrup
395 Riverside Drive
New York, New York 10025
   Comments: Batik is an Indonesian textile-printing
            method of using wax to coat parts of the
            material that are not to be dyed.

Society of North American Goldsmiths
2849 Saint Ann Drive
Greenbay, Wisconsin 54301
   Comments: Goldsmiths, silversmiths, jewelers.

Sumi-E Society of America
4200 Kings Mill Lane
Annandale, Virginia 22003
   Comments: Oriental brush-painting.

Ukiyo-E Society of America
1692 Second Avenue
New York, New York 10028
   Comments: Japanese woodblock prints.

Chapter 7

Newspapers

Local newspapers contain a wealth of possibilities for locating resources within the community. A creative approach to scanning articles and containing promising leads can be very effective.

All newspapers print more than just international, national, state, and local news. They also run human interest stories which spotlight a variety of individuals and groups. These individuals are not necessarily involved in activities of great societal significance; their activities, talents, or interests are simply unique or notable in some way that makes for entertaining reading. Many of these individuals and groups can add a great deal to the geriatric program through their involvement.

Interesting groups and individuals who are not confined solely to metropolitan areas; consequently, articles about such people are not restricted to major newspapers. In fact, smaller towns are more likely to need and to print this type of human interest story. Therefore, both major *and* local community or special interest newspapers should be checked.

Local human interest articles are usually not located in the first or main section of the newspaper; this section is usually reserved for "hard" national and international news.

The human interest articles are generally found in lifestyle sections which deal with health, culinary, beauty, and fashion topics, or in sections which are devoted to local news and events.

While a few of the articles may give the individual's or group's address/phone number, most do not. Addresses and phone numbers may be printed for businesses and organizations, but seldom for individuals who are not affiliated with a business or club. It is the interested reader's responsibility to locate the individual's address or phone number by using the phone book.

Using the newspaper to find and develop community resources is not a one-shot endeavor. Newspapers will seldom yield more than one possibility each day. Sometimes weeks or even months can go by until a promising lead occurs. Program planners need to cultivate the habit of scanning the paper on a daily basis to look for leads.

Every community has its own unique individuals, activities, and associations. The following examples are offered for illustrative purposes only. They are based on actual articles which appeared in newspapers in several different small towns and large cities. The leads provided by these articles resulted in some very successful programming. A large number of the individuals and groups became involved with the author's geriatric programs on a regular basis.

- A group of senior citizens who formed a "kitchen band" (utilizing common household objects such as washboards and spoons) gave a concert.
- A collector of Civil War artifacts lectured on his collection.
- A woman who directs fashion shows which feature elderly models gave a fashion show with some of the participants actually serving as models.
- A man with a record collection of over a thousand albums of all types put together several highly entertaining topical shows such as "Music from Broadway Plays," "Irish Folk Music," and "Music of the 1920's."

- Members of a poetry group were willing to come to the geriatric facility and give poetry readings.
- Members of the cast of a high school play came to the geriatric facility to practice a condensed version of the play.
- Impersonators of famous entertainers (such as Mae West and Michael Jackson) performed at the geriatric program.
- A husband and wife who have been dancing together for fifty years were able to give a very professional ballroom dancing demonstration.
- A blind pianist in his twenties, who had mistakenly been diagnosed as mentally retarded for much of his life but later was found to be hearing impaired, gave weekly classical music recitals.
- A store which sells and provides instruction in musical instruments advertised a class for preschool children to learn to play the violin. Several months later, the students gave a recital.
- A harmonica group (with all members at least seventy years old) was willing to give concerts at a nursing home several times a year.
- A bottle collector with over 500 types of unique bottles brought over one hundred bottles to the facility and gave a fascinating talk about their origins and how they were acquired.
- A man who makes handmade wooden musical instruments demonstrated his craft and played his instruments.
- A woman exhibited her "shell art" (objects made with and decorated by shells).
- An orchid grower exhibited and discussed over fifty varieties of orchids and later returned to help participants start an orchid growing group.
- A man who plays classical music on a saw gave a concert.
- A fortune teller/astrologist told people's fortunes by reading palms.
- A harpist performed at the geriatric facility.
- A couple who have travelled around the world gave a travelogue.

Chapter 8

ACTIVITY PREPARATION
WORK SHEETS

The work sheets in this chapter offer a concise but comprehensive means of organizing data about community resources. Each page features a different activity, along with the community resource (individual or group) which could sponsor or help with that activity. Space is provided for the actual name, address, and phone number of the community resource; this information is to be filled in as indicated.

Possible needs for materials and supplies are briefly listed, as is the type of physical environment which is most appropriate for that activity. Some activities need formal seating (all chairs neatly lined up in rows, with the lecturer at front) whereas others are best held under informal circumstances to promote mingling among the participants. Some activities need to be held outdoors, while others require a special area such as kitchen facilities.

The total number of participants refers to the appropriateness of large or small groups for the activity in question.

The category of restrictions refers to any factors which might indicate that certain individuals should either not participate or else be closely monitored during the activity. Such factors might include medical problems, confusion, or poor motor skills.

Whenever possible, outside participation from the community at large should be elicited. The type of population to be invited to join in the activity depends on the actual activity. In some circumstances, the number of participants should be fairly low and outside participation should not be sought.

Each work sheet has space for additional comments to be written as the activity planner deems appropriate.

Several blank sheets have been provided for other activities which are not mentioned in the text.

ACTIVITY PREPARATION WORK SHEET

Activity:
Discussions and displays of antiques

Community Resource:
Antique dealers
Name:
Address:

Phone number:

Materials Needed:
Tables to display antiques
Microphone

Physical Environment:
Informal or formal seating with display tables at front of the room

Ideal Number of Participants:
Any number, although smaller groups will ensure that each participant gets a chance to closely view antiques

Restrictions Precluding Participation:
Participants who are confused or have poor coordination should not be permitted to handle antiques

Outside Participation:
People of all ages in the community who are interested in antiques

Comments:

ACTIVITY PREPARATION WORK SHEET

Activity:
Art appreciation lecture

Community Resource:
Art dealers and consultants
Owners/employees from art galleries
Name:
Address:

Phone number:

Materials Needed:
Microphone
(possibly a slide projector)

Physical Environment:
Informal or formal seating

Ideal Number of Participants:
Any number, although smaller groups will ensure a better view for each participant

Restrictions Precluding Participation:
None

Outside Participation:
Members of the community who are interested in art

Comments:

ACTIVITY PREPARATION WORK SHEET

Activity:
Artists-at-work demonstrations

Community Resource:
Teachers and students from art classes
Name:
Address:

Phone number:

Materials Needed:
Artists will usually provide own materials but may need some tables to work on

Physical Environment:
Informal seating where participants can mingle with the artists

Ideal Number of Participants:
Small to medium sized groups

Restrictions Precluding Participation:
None

Outside Participation:
Outside members of the community who are interested in watching the demonstrations

Comments:

ACTIVITY PREPARATION WORK SHEET

Activity:
Astrological lectures
Fortune telling
Horoscope reading

Community Resource:
Astrologers
Fortune tellers
Name:
Address:

Phone number:

Materials Needed:
Microphone
(May need a chalk board for astrological lectures)

Physical Environment:
Formal seating with lecturer at front

Ideal Number of Participants:
Any number, although smaller groups mean that more participants will have a chance to have their horoscope read

Restrictions Precluding Participation:
None

Outside Participation:
Interested members of community

Comments:

ACTIVITY PREPARATION WORK SHEET

Activity:
Auctions

Community Resource:
Auctioneers
Name:
Address:

Phone number:

Materials Needed:
Microphone
Display tables
Items to be auctioned

Physical Environment:
Formal or informal seating

Ideal Number of Participants:
Any number

Restrictions Precluding Participation:
Participants who have impaired hearing or vision should be seated in the front

Outside Participation:
The general public

Comments:

ACTIVITY PREPARATION WORK SHEET

Activity:
Audiological lectures and testing

Community Resource:
Audiologists
Name:
Address:

Phone number:

Materials Needed:
Microphone for lecture
Tables for testing equipment

Physical Environment:
For lecture, formal seating environment with lecturer in front

For testing, a quiet, private room

Ideal Number of Participants:
Any number for lecture

For testing, the number of participants may need to be limited

Restrictions Precluding Participation:
None, although a physician's referral or prescription may be needed

Outside Participation:
Interested members of the community

Comments:

ACTIVITY PREPARATION WORK SHEET

Activity:
Baking demonstration

Community Resource:
Bakers
Name:
Address:

Phone number:

Materials Needed:
Baker or facility may provide the ingredients and supplies according to the baker's wishes

Physical Environment:
Informal seating around tables for the preparation of pastries. Demonstration may need to be held (at least partially) in the kitchen

Ideal Number of Participants:
Any number, although smaller groups allow for greater participation

Restrictions Precluding Participation:
Diabetics need to be carefully monitored when baked goods are sampled

Outside Participation:
Outside community might be invited to bake sale

Comments:

ACTIVITY PREPARATION WORK SHEET

Activity:
 Bartending lecture/demonstration
 Cocktail party

Community Resource:
 Bartenders
 Name:
 Address:

 Phone number:

Materials Needed:
 Tables to serve as work area for bartender; may need to be by an electrical outlet to plug in the blender.

 Bartender or facility will need to furnish ingredients and glasses, depending on bartender's wishes.

 Hors d'ouevres may be served

Physical Environment:
 Informal seating

Ideal Number of Participants:
 Any number

Restrictions Precluding Participation:
 Physician's approval may be necessary for consumption of alcoholic beverages

Outside Participation:
 None

Comments:

ACTIVITY PREPARATION WORK SHEET

Activity:
Beer making

Community Resource:
Owners/managers of home-brewing stores
Name:
Address:

Phone number:

Materials Needed:
Usually furnished by instructor

Physical Environment:
Informal seating arrangements

Ideal Number of Participants:
Any number

Restrictions Precluding Participation:
A doctor's approval may be necessary for participation

Outside Participation:
Interested members of community

Comments:

ACTIVITY PREPARATION WORK SHEET

Activity:
Cake decorating

Community Resource:
Cake decorators
Owners/employees of cake decorating stores
Name:
Address:

Phone number:

Materials Needed:
Tables to serve as work area
Decorators should bring decorating supplies.
Program may need to furnish cakes.

Physical Environment:
Informal seating, with audience circulating around tables to see decorated cakes

Ideal Number of Participants:
Any number

Restrictions Precluding Participation:
Diabetics need to be carefully monitored in terms of sampling baked goods

Outside Participation:
Interested members of the community might be invited to the demonstration and subsequent bake sale

Comments:

ACTIVITY PREPARATION WORK SHEET

Activity:
Calligraphy demonstration/instruction

Community Resource:
Professional calligrapher
Name:
Address:

Phone number:

Materials Needed:
Tables

Supplies (ink and paper) to be furnished by calligrapher
or program

Physical Environment:
Informal seating at tables

Ideal Number of Participants:
Small groups

Restrictions Precluding Participation:
None, although calligraphy does require a significant
degree of eye-hand coordination and fine-motor dexterity

Outside Participation:
None

Comments:

ACTIVITY PREPARATION WORK SHEET

Activity:
 Candy making

Community Resource:
 Owners/managers of retail businesses which sell supplies for candy making.
 Name:
 Address:

 Phone number:

Materials Needed:
 Tables for work areas
 Instructor will usually provide supplies

Physical Environment:
 Informal seating

Ideal Number of Participants:
 Any number

Restrictions Precluding Participation:
 Diabetics need to be carefully monitored

Outside Participation:
 Members of the community might be invited to purchase candy

Comments:

ACTIVITY PREPARATION WORK SHEET

Activity:
Ceramics

Community Resource:
Ceramics instructor
Name:
Address:

Phone number:

Materials Needed:
Instructor to furnish supplies and greenware

Physical Environment:
Seating at tables

Ideal Number of Participants:
Small group

Restrictions Precluding Participation:
None

Outside Participation:
None

Comments:

ACTIVITY PREPARATION WORK SHEET

Activity:
Chinese cooking demonstration/instruction

Community Resource:
Chinese cooking instructors
Name:
Address:

Phone number:

Materials Needed:
Table as work area
Cooking utensils, pans, woks
Food as needed

Physical Environment:
Informal seating, possibly in kitchen

Ideal Number of Participants:
Any number

Restrictions Precluding Participation:
Dietary restrictions need to be observed

Outside Participation:
Family and community members

Comments:

ACTIVITY PREPARATION WORK SHEET

Activity:
Coin collecting lecture and exhibit

Community Resource:
Coin collectors
Coin dealers
Name:
Address:

Phone number:

Materials Needed:
Microphone

Physical Environment:
Informal or formal seating

Ideal Number of Participants:
Any number

Restrictions Precluding Participation:
None

Outside Participation:
Interested members of community, including history or
social studies classes

Comments:

ACTIVITY PREPARATION WORK SHEET

Activity:
Color consultation lectures

Community Resource:
Color consultants
Name:
Address:

Phone number:

Materials Needed:
Microphone
Possibly slide projectors, chalk board

Physical Environment:
Informal seating, with lecturer at front

Ideal Number of Participants:
Any number

Restrictions Precluding Participation:
None

Outside Participation:
Interested members of community

Comments:

ACTIVITY PREPARATION WORK SHEET

Activity:
Computer demonstration/lecture

Community Resource:
Computer programmers
Computer dealers
Name:
Address:

Phone number:

Materials Needed:
Computers to be furnished by lecturer
Microphone

Physical Environment:
Informal seating, accessible to computers

Ideal Number of Participants:
Any number, although smaller groups will ensure that more participants will actually get to experience the computers first-hand

Restrictions Precluding Participation:
None

Outside Participation:
None

Comments:

ACTIVITY PREPARATION WORK SHEET

Activity:
Crafts instruction

Community Resource:
Instructors from craft supply stores
Name:
Address:

Phone number:

Materials Needed:
Depends on craft

Physical Environment:
Seating at tables

Ideal Number of Participants:
Any number

Restrictions Precluding Participation:
Visual or fine-motor impairment may preclude participation in certain crafts

Outside Participation:
Interested members of community

Comments:

ACTIVITY PREPARATION WORK SHEET

Activity:
Dance lessons

Community Resource:
Students and teachers from dance schools
Name:
Address:

Phone number:

Materials Needed:
Record player

Physical Environment:
Floor space conducive to dancing

Ideal Number of Participants:
Any number

Restrictions Precluding Participation:
Postural instability and orthopedic problems

Outside Participation:
Interested members of community

Comments:

ACTIVITY PREPARATION WORK SHEET

Activity:
Dance recitals

Community Resource:
Students and teachers from dance studios
Name:
Address:

Phone number:

Materials Needed:
Record player

Physical Environment:
Need floor space conducive to dancing
Formal seating

Ideal Number of Participants:
Any number

Restrictions Precluding Participation:
None

Outside Participation:
Interested members of community

Comments:

ACTIVITY PREPARATION WORK SHEET

Activity:
Lectures on doll collecting and repairing

Community Resource:
Employees/owners of doll hospitals or toy stores
Name:
Address:

Phone number:

Materials Needed:
Microphone

Physical Environment:
Formal seating, with provisions made for participants to view the dolls up close

Ideal Number of Participants:
Any number

Restrictions Precluding Participation:
None

Outside Participation:
Interested members of community, especially children

Comments:

ACTIVITY PREPARATION WORK SHEET

Activity:
Entertainment

Community Resource:
Professional entertainers
School groups
Church groups
Name:
Address:

Phone number:

Materials Needed:
Generally just a microphone

Physical Environment:
Depending on event, formal or informal seating

Ideal Number of Participants:
Any number

Restrictions Precluding Participation:
None, but participants with impaired vision/hearing
should be seated in front

Outside Participation:
Members of the community

Comments:

ACTIVITY PREPARATION WORK SHEET

Activity:
Ethnic dances, music, lectures, films, and cuisine

Community Resource:
Ethnic groups
Name:
Address:

Phone number:

Materials Needed:
Depends on program

Physical Environment:
Depends on program

Ideal Number of Participants:
Depends on environment

Restrictions Precluding Participation:
None, except for individual dietary restrictions if food is
served

Outside Participation:
Depends on program

Comments:

ACTIVITY PREPARATION WORK SHEET

Activity:
Exercise sessions

Community Resource:
Representatives from health or fitness clubs
Name:
Address:

Phone number:

Materials Needed:
Possibly a microphone, record player, other materials, depending on instructor's wishes

Physical Environment:
Seating in a circular arrangement

Ideal Number of Participants:
Any number

Restrictions Precluding Participation:
Cardiovascular and orthopedic problems may restrict participation. Consultation with the nurse or occupational/physical therapist may be indicated, and a physician's approval may be necessary.

Outside Participation:
Older members of community

Comments:

ACTIVITY PREPARATION WORK SHEET

Activity:
Eyeglass frame fashion show and try-on session

Community Resource:
Optical goods dealer
Name:
Address:

Phone number:

Materials Needed:
Mirrors
Optical goods dealer will bring eyeglass frames

Physical Environment:
Informal seating at tables

Ideal Number of Participants:
Small group

Restrictions Precluding Participation:
None

Outside Participation:
None

Comments:

ACTIVITY PREPARATION WORK SHEET

Activity:
Fashion shows

Community Resource:
Modeling schools
Clothing stores
Name:
Address:

Phone number:

Materials Needed:
Microphone

Physical Environment:
Formal or informal seating, with a cleared area to serve
as a runway for models

Ideal Number of Participants:
Any number

Restrictions Precluding Participation:
None

Outside Participation:
Family members

Comments:

ACTIVITY PREPARATION WORK SHEET

Activity:
Financial seminars/lectures

Community Resource:
Accountants
Stockbrokers
Financial planners
Name:
Address:

Phone number:

Materials Needed:
Paper and pencils to be furnished to the participants to write down anonymous questions.

Microphone

Physical Environment:
Formal seating arrangement with lecturer in front

Ideal Number of Participants:
Any number

Restrictions Precluding Participation:
None

Outside Participation:
Senior members of the community

Comments:

ACTIVITY PREPARATION WORK SHEET

Activity:
　Flower arranging

Community Resource:
　Florists
　Name:
　Address:

　Phone number:

Materials Needed:
　Flowers and other supplies furnished by florist

Physical Environment:
　Seating at tables

Ideal Number of Participants:
　Any number

Restrictions Precluding Participation:
　None (except for hay fever!)

Outside Participation:
　Family and community members

Comments:

ACTIVITY PREPARATION WORK SHEET

Activity:
Friendly visits, special parties, and other social activities

Community Resource:
Civic service groups
Church groups
Schools
Day care centers and nurseries
Name:
Address:

Phone number:

Materials Needed:
None for visits; refreshments for parties

Physical Environment:
Informal; does not need to be pre-arranged

Ideal Number of Participants:
For visits, the number of geriatric participants that is equivalent to the number of volunteers, thus enabling one-on-one relationships.

For parties, the number of participants that is conducive to mingling with the volunteers.

Restrictions Precluding Participation:
None, except that diabetics need to be closely monitored in terms of refreshments

Outside Participation:
None

Comments:

ACTIVITY PREPARATION WORK SHEET

Activity:
Hair cutting, styling, coloring
Skin care
Makeup application/demonstration

Community Resource:
Barbers
Beauticians
Students from beauty culture schools
Name:
Address:

Phone number:

Materials Needed:
Supplies as requested or furnished by the beautician

Physical Environment:
Working areas/tables/chairs/sinks

Ideal Number of Participants:
Should be in proportion with the number of beauticians

Restrictions Precluding Participation:
Certain skin conditions, as noted by the nurse or physician

Outside Participation:
None

Comments:

ACTIVITY PREPARATION WORK SHEET

Activity:
Handwriting analysis

Community Resource:
Handwriting expert
Name:
Address:

Phone number:

Materials Needed:
Samples of participants' handwriting
Microphone
Chalkboard

Physical Environment:
Formal seating arrangement with lecturer at front

Ideal Number of Participants:
Any number

Restrictions Precluding Participation:
None

Outside Participation:
Family members and interested members of the community

Comments:

ACTIVITY PREPARATION WORK SHEET

Activity:
Health lectures

Community Resource:
Health associations
Professionals
Name:
Address:

Phone number:

Materials Needed:
Microphone
Chalkboard

Physical Environment:
Formal seating arrangements with lecturer at front

Ideal Number of Participants:
Any number

Restrictions Precluding Participation:
None

Outside Participation:
Interested members of community

Comments:

ACTIVITY PREPARATION WORK SHEET

Activity:
  Human relations lecture

Community Resource:
  Human relations counselors
  Psychiatrists
  Psychologists
  Social workers
  Name:
  Address:

  Phone number:

Materials Needed:
  Microphone

Physical Environment:
  Formal seating with lecturer at front

Ideal Number of Participants:
  Any number

Restrictions Precluding Participation:
  None

Outside Participation:
  Interested community members

Comments:

ACTIVITY PREPARATION WORK SHEET

Activity:
Karate and other martial arts demonstrations

Community Resource:
Instructors and students of the martial arts
Name:
Address:

Phone number:

Materials Needed:
None

Physical Environment:
Formal seating arrangement, with enough space in front
for demonstration

Ideal Number of Participants:
Any number

Restrictions Precluding Participation:
None

Outside Participation:
Interested members of community

Comments:

ACTIVITY PREPARATION WORK SHEET

Activity:
Legal lecture

Community Resource:
Attorneys
Name:
Address:

Phone number:

Materials Needed:
Microphone

Paper and pens for participants to write anonymous questions

Physical Environment:
Formal seating arrangement with lecturer at front

Ideal Number of Participants:
Any number

Restrictions Precluding Participation:
None

Outside Participation:
Interested senior members of community

Comments:

ACTIVITY PREPARATION WORK SHEET

Activity:
Magic shows and instruction

Community Resource:
Magicians
Name:
Address:

Phone number:

Materials Needed:
Microphone
Magician will usually furnish props

Physical Environment:
Formal or informal seating arrangements with accessible view of magician

Ideal Number of Participants:
Any number

Restrictions Precluding Participation:
None

Outside Participation:
Children of staff members and relatives; local school-children

Comments:

ACTIVITY PREPARATION WORK SHEET

Activity:
Makeup applications
Lectures about makeup and skin care
Makeup lessons

Community Resource:
Cosmeticians from drug stores and beauty salons
Representatives of national cosmetic companies
Name:
Address:

Phone number:

Materials Needed:
Mirrors
Cosmetics to be supplied by companies
Cleansing creams, tissues, cotton balls

Physical Environment:
For lecture, formal seating with lecturer at front

For makeup lessons and applications, seating at long tables

Ideal Number of Participants:
A fairly small group to enable all to participate in makeup applications and skin care

Restrictions Precluding Participation:
Skin conditions which preclude the use of cosmetics

Outside Participation:
None

Comments:

ACTIVITY PREPARATION WORK SHEET

Activity:
Manicures

Community Resource:
Professional manicurist
Name:
Address:

Phone number:

Materials Needed:
Manicurist will probably bring supplies

Physical Environment:
Seating at tables

Ideal Number of Participants:
Small groups

Restrictions Precluding Participation:
Certain skin conditions or metabolic diseases, as determined by nurse or physician

Outside Participation:
None

Comments:

ACTIVITY PREPARATION WORK SHEET

Activity:
Exhibits and lectures from museums

Community Resource:
Museum employees
Name:
Address:

Phone number:

Materials Needed:
Microphone
Display table

Physical Environment:
Accessible seating to display tables

Ideal Number of Participants:
Any number

Restrictions Precluding Participation:
None

Outside Participation:
Children from nearby schools

Comments:

ACTIVITY PREPARATION WORK SHEET

Activity:
Music recitals
Music instruction

Community Resource:
Students or instructors of instrumental/vocal music
Name:
Address:

Phone number:

Materials Needed:
Microphone

Physical Environment:
Informal seating

Ideal Number of Participants:
Any number

Restrictions Precluding Participation:
None

Outside Participation:
General public

Comments:

ACTIVITY PREPARATION WORK SHEET

Activity:
　Pet visitations

Community Resource:
　Humane societies
　Pet stores
　Name:
　Address:

　Phone number:

Materials Needed:
　None

Physical Environment:
　Informal seating arrangements

Ideal Number of Participants:
　Small groups to ensure that all participants get to mingle with animals

Restrictions Precluding Participation:
　Allergies to animals
　Fear of animals

Outside Participation:
　None

Comments:

ACTIVITY PREPARATION WORK SHEET

Activity:
Plant lectures

Community Resource:
Employees of greenhouses, nurseries, and plant stores
Name:
Address:

Phone number:

Materials Needed:
Soil, watering can, plants (needs to be coordinated with lecturer)

Physical Environment:
Outdoor gardening area or seating at indoor tables

Ideal Number of Participants:
Any number

Restrictions Precluding Participation:
None

Outside Participation:
Family or community members, Garden Clubs

Comments:

ACTIVITY PREPARATION WORK SHEET

Activity:
Portrait sessions

Community Resource:
Teachers and students from art classes
Name:
Address:

Phone number:

Materials Needed:
Artists will usually provide own materials but may need some tables to work on

Physical Environment:
Informal seating

Ideal Number of Participants:
Only a limited number will be able to have their portraits done

Restrictions Precluding Participation:
None

Outside Participation:
Family members

Comments:

ACTIVITY PREPARATION WORK SHEET

Activity:
Religious services or studies

Community Resource:
Church groups
Name:
Address:

Phone number:

Materials Needed:
May need microphone, piano, organ

Physical Environment:
Formal seating arrangement, with leader in front of audience

Ideal Number of Participants:
Any number

Restrictions Precluding Participation:
None

Outside Participation:
Interested members of community

Comments:

ACTIVITY PREPARATION WORK SHEET

Activity:
Relaxation/biofeedback therapy

Community Resource:
Biofeedback therapists
Psychologists
Physical therapists
Name:
Address:

Phone number:

Materials Needed:
Depends on therapist, but usually a microphone or record player

Physical Environment:
Informal seating

Ideal Number of Participants:
Small groups

Restrictions Precluding Participation:
Usually none (since the therapy is quite safe) but a physician's approval may be necessary

Outside Participation:
None

Comments:

ACTIVITY PREPARATION WORK SHEET

Activity:
Special interest lectures

Community Resource:
Special interest groups
Name:
Address:

Phone number:

Materials Needed:
Depends on program

Physical Environment:
Depends on program

Ideal Number of Participants:
Depends on program

Restrictions Precluding Participation:
Usually none

Outside Participation:
Depends on program; usually interested members of the community can be invited

Comments:

ACTIVITY PREPARATION WORK SHEET

Activity:
   Square dancing

Community Resource:
   Square dance club
   Name:
   Address:

   Phone number:

Materials Needed:
   Microphone
   Record player
   Records to be furnished by square dancers

Physical Environment:
   Informal seating, with large space cleared in front or center of room

Ideal Number of Participants:
   Any number

Restrictions Precluding Participation:
   None; even wheelchair bound individuals can participate

Outside Participation:
   Family members

Comments:

ACTIVITY PREPARATION WORK SHEET

Activity:
Stamp collecting

Community Resource:
Stamp collectors
Employees/owners of stamp collecting stores
Name:
Address:

Phone number:

Materials Needed:
Microphone

Physical Environment:
Informal seating

Ideal Number of Participants:
Any number

Restrictions Precluding Participation:
None

Outside Participation:
History or geography classes from local schools

Comments:

ACTIVITY PREPARATION WORK SHEET

Activity:
Travelogues

Community Resource:
Travel agencies
Name:
Address:

Phone number:

Materials Needed:
Movie screen
Microphone

Physical Environment:
Formal seating with screen in front of room

Ideal Number of Participants:
Any number

Restrictions Precluding Participation:
None

Outside Participation:
General public

Comments:

ACTIVITY PREPARATION WORK SHEET

Activity:

Community Resource:

   Name:
   Address:

   Phone number:

Materials Needed:

Physical Environment:

Ideal Number of Participants:

Restrictions Precluding Participation:

Outside Participation:

Comments:

ACTIVITY PREPARATION WORK SHEET

Activity:

Community Resource:

   Name:
   Address:

   Phone number:

Materials Needed:

Physical Environment:

Ideal Number of Participants:

Restrictions Precluding Participation:

Outside Participation:

Comments:

ACTIVITY PREPARATION WORK SHEET

Activity:

Community Resource:

    Name:
    Address:

    Phone number:

Materials Needed:

Physical Environment:

Ideal Number of Participants:

Restrictions Precluding Participation:

Outside Participation:

Comments:

ACTIVITY PREPARATION WORK SHEET

Activity:

Community Resource:

Name:
Address:
Phone number:

Materials Needed:

Physical Environment:

Ideal Number of Participants:

Restrictions Precluding Participation:

Outside Participation:

Comments:

ACTIVITY PREPARATION WORK SHEET

Activity:

Community Resource:

> *Name:*
> *Address:*
> *Phone number:*

Materials Needed:

Physical Environment:

Ideal Number of Participants:

Restrictions Precluding Participation:

Outside Participation:

Comments:

ACTIVITY PREPARATION WORK SHEET

Activity:

Community Resource:

Name:
Address:
Phone number:

Materials Needed:

Physical Environment:

Ideal Number of Participants:

Restrictions Precluding Participation:

Outside Participation:

Comments:

ACTIVITY PREPARATION WORK SHEET

Activity:

Community Resource:

   Name:
   Address:
   Phone number:

Materials Needed:

Physical Environment:

Ideal Number of Participants:

Restrictions Precluding Participation:

Outside Participation:

Comments:

ACTIVITY PREPARATION WORK SHEET

Activity:

Community Resource:

Name:
Address:

Phone number:

Materials Needed:

Physical Environment:

Ideal Number of Participants:

Restrictions Precluding Participation:

Outside Participation:

Comments:

ACTIVITY PREPARATION WORK SHEET

Activity:

Community Resource:

> *Name:*
> *Address:*
>
> *Phone number:*

Materials Needed:

Physical Environment:

Ideal Number of Participants:

Restrictions Precluding Participation:

Outside Participation:

Comments:

ACTIVITY PREPARATION WORK SHEET

Activity:

Community Resource:

Name:
Address:
Phone number:

Materials Needed:

Physical Environment:

Ideal Number of Participants:

Restrictions Precluding Participation:

Outside Participation:

Comments:

ACTIVITY PREPARATION WORK SHEET

Activity:

Community Resource:

 Name:
 Address:

 Phone number:

Materials Needed:

Physical Environment:

Ideal Number of Participants:

Restrictions Precluding Participation:

Outside Participation:

Comments:

INDEX